What the  Amish Can Teach Us About the Simple Life

What the  Amish Can Teach Us About the Simple Life

GEORGIA VAROZZA

HARVEST HOUSE PUBLISHERS
EUGENE, OREGON

Cover design by Garborg Design Works, Minneapolis, Minnesota

Cover photos © Chris Garborg; Bigstock

Neither the author nor the publisher assumes any liability for possible adverse consequences as a result of the information contained herein.

WHAT THE AMISH CAN TEACH US ABOUT THE SIMPLE LIFE
Copyright © 2013 by Georgia Varozza
Published by Harvest House Publishers
Eugene, Oregon 97402
www.HarvestHousePublishers.com

Library of Congress Cataloging-in-Publication Data
    Varozza, Georgia.
    What the Amish can teach us about the simple life / Georgia Varozza.
       p. cm.
    ISBN 978-0-7369-5260-6 (pbk.)
    ISBN 978-0-73-69-5261-3 (eBook)
    1. Conduct of life. 2. Amish—Conduct of life. 3. Mennonites—Conduct of life. I. Title.
    BJ1581.2.V37 2013
    248.4'8973—dc23

                                        2012030034

Printed in the United States of America

13 14 15 16 17 18 19 20 / VP-KG / 10 9 8 7 6 5 4 3 2 1

To my family.
You cheerfully put up with my many experiments
and (almost!) never complained.
May the Lord bless you and keep you,
and may you walk with Him always.
I love you all.

◆ ◆ ◆ ◆ ◆

To Paula.
In our happy quest to care for our families,
we've tried just about everything.
We are definitely two peas in a pod!

◆ ◆ ◆ ◆ ◆

And to Nick Harrison.
You gave me the encouragement I needed to
enlarge the place of my tent (Isaiah 54:2).
I am blessed to know you.

Contents

A Simple Life Revealed

I have a vivid recollection of my "plain" aunties (great aunts, really) coming to visit when I was a young child. They were solid farm women with prayer caps on their heads and demurely patterned dresses. They treated me kindly and laughed a lot with my mother. They helped me embroider my first project—a pillowcase that had a design of two squirrels running up a branch. I picked out the pattern all by myself (I must have been about seven at the time), and I thought it was lovely.

I have another memory from this time, but it isn't nearly as positive. A boy from my school (I was in second grade) teased me during recess about those "stupid Amish," only he mispronounced it "Ay-mish." The only defense I knew was to tell him he was saying "Amish" wrong and he didn't know anything.

I grew up learning about the Amish and other plain Anabaptists decades before some of the communities became tourist attractions. I admired their industriousness and simple lifestyles. Even as a youngster I wanted to emulate those qualities. In fact, I remember being teased for years about being born a hundred years too late. I didn't mind the teasing at all because I quite agreed.

To help make ends meet when I went away to college, I made quilts, embroidered shirts, and crocheted afghans that I sold to my fellow students. For a time I lived in a third-floor walk-up in San Francisco. Though I was surrounded by a city's worth of concrete and high-rises, I still managed to garden—on the fire escape. I'd climb out my kitchen window and grab a handful of herbs or a bit of lettuce or spinach for a meal, never once stopping to think this might seem odd to other city dwellers.

When I was preparing to get married, my gift list gave my poor mother fits. I didn't have a china pattern or list of linens and fancy gadgets our guests could use as a guide. No, my list consisted of such things as a pressure canner, canning jars (as many as anyone cared to buy!), a wheelbarrow, a tiller, and a garden spade, just to name a few. And when my husband and I shopped for our first home, I didn't really care what the house looked like. It was the dirt that surrounded the house that grabbed my attention. After all, a house could be fixed, but the land is forever.

When our children were young, we attended a conservative Amish–Mennonite church in the area. I dressed plain (made from a homemade pattern supplied by one of my church sisters) and wore a head covering. In their quiet way, the women of the church accepted me, and I developed happy friendships with a number of them. Together we harvested and canned produce from our gardens and shared recipes and housekeeping tips. We ate together and visited while the children played outside. I fondly recall a tradition several of the families had. After eating, while the adults were yet seated and visiting, the children would stand behind us and gently massage our necks. What a lovely way to end a meal! This gave the grown-ups a chance for one last cup of coffee or sun tea before we women popped up to do the dishes and the men wandered off to discuss whatever was of current interest.

Church services were a hushed and holy affair. We would silently enter the sanctuary; women seated on the left, and men seated on the right. Hymns were sung a cappella, and at the beginning of each verse the songster would lead in. The congregation always paused before beginning to sing along. Everyone knew the hymn by heart, but that show of humility was the way things were done. The minister delivered his sermon with a quiet earnestness that spoke to my heart, and praying was done on our knees, heads bowed, our faces covered by our hands.

There were also work frolics, when the women would gather in the basement of the church to piece and tie comforters for those less fortunate. In the summer there was Bible school for the children, and in October, revival meetings took place every evening for an entire week. Visiting ministers would speak, and the faithful were exhorted to honor Christ in all things and to live lives reflective of the Savior's redeeming work.

In many ways, those were halcyon days for our family. We spent our time close to home, busy with the work of living. We eschewed television, radio, and electronic games and gadgets. If we wanted to have fun, we made it ourselves. My children were full of creative ideas for play, and they spent many hours outside just being kids.

My twin sister, Paula, and her children lived nearby. We joined forces often as our days unfolded. Our kids were very close, and cousin squabbles were thankfully few and far between. Paula and I had plenty of time to work together on the tasks of the day and season. Processing and canning 40 quarts of tomato sauce in one day? Not a problem. Picking and freezing gallons and gallons of blueberries from my 53 blueberry bushes? Enjoyable. My sister and I worked together, and we truly experienced the adage that many hands make light work.

Both of us had an insatiable curiosity coupled with a strong desire to care for our families. We attempted many projects together over the years. Some were unmitigated disasters, like the time we decided we would only scythe the grain we grew. That didn't last long because we quickly discovered it was extremely hard work, took a lot of time, and required much skill. But other projects were grand successes so we've incorporated them into our routines.

Greater still are the sweet memories I have of pitching in together to accomplish the tasks at hand. The joy of working collectively to lighten the load was a reality for us. My sister and I drew even closer during those busy years of raising our families. This was a very important form of community for us, and it worked beautifully. We learned to work in concert, and by dividing the chores we were able to accomplish much more than we ever could have alone. And as we worked and played and visited, as we clothed and fed our families with the industrious work of our hands, as we studied God's Word and tuned our hearts to hear His voice, we were teaching our children these precious lessons as well—not so much with words, but by the testimony of our daily lives as we discharged our duties with cheerfulness and the pleasure of jobs well done.

Few get to experience that type of community, that kind of contentment, that kind of joy. The world is busy luring us into believing we can't live without whatever they're selling and telling us we must get ahead and make more money. We're told that our children will be left behind if we don't provide them with every possible advantage, and we'd better begin when they're babies or it will be too late. We're shown by constant advertisements that we need to take exotic vacations and drive the latest models of luxury cars. We're advised to get a college education and instructed that home ownership in the "right" neighborhood is a must.

To attain all this, we must work, work, work. We not only need to pay for this lifestyle, but we'd better have a hefty retirement fund growing in a diversified portfolio for our golden years or we're sunk.

The truth is there is another way. We can slow down—"come home" in the finest sense of the word *home*. We can consciously delineate between our needs and our wants, and then make informed and prayerful decisions about what we will allow into our lives. We can concentrate on our families, friendships, and faith communities instead of racing through life being too busy to deepen our most precious relationships.

We can honor our families, especially our children, by spending quality *and* quantity time with them. Instead of relying only on evening hours when everyone is tired after a long day, we can build in time when we and our children are fresh, energetic, and excited about spending active time together. We can let our families know we love them, enjoy being with them, and that we believe family members need to support each other through thick and thin.

I believe that by looking to the Amish lifestyle for inspiration, we can discover tips and ideas for creating a better future for our families and ourselves. Because they've chosen "plain" living for so long, we can learn key ways to forgo some of this world's enticements and gain more time and freedom to love our families, tend to our homes, and serve in our communities. Abundance can be found in living simply.

My prayer is that you will come away from reading this book excited about making some changes to help your family live more simply. I hope this book will provide the impetus for your family to begin a dialogue about what is really important in your lives and how to achieve it. I believe that what we do can influence people today and for generations. None of us live in a vacuum. Our actions produce reactions, and our lives matter. God says we are "fearfully and wonderfully made" and that His "works" (that's you and me!) are wonderful (Psalm 139:14). We need to share that loving and hopeful message!

There is a multitude of ideas for creating a simple, homemade life between the pages of this book. I hope you'll find many ideas that resonate with you and encourage you to say, "Yes! We can do that!" May God's richest blessings be yours.

Why the Amish?

The Amish have an enduring appeal for many of us. From the outside looking in, we view their way of life with great curiosity. What about them draws us in and causes us to want something similar for our families and our own lives?

The first things we notice are the way they dress and their horse-and-buggy mode of transportation. They don't care about the latest fashions, and they don't speed to their destinations at 60 miles per hour—seeing nothing along the way because they're focused on getting there in a hurry. We look longingly at their neat farms with solid houses and barns and large vegetable gardens. We enjoy the farm animals that dot the landscape and fields of corn and hay ripening in the summer heat. When evening comes, we see their homes lit by the soft glow of kerosene or gas lanterns. If the night air is chilly, smoke curling from a chimney indicates a woodstove is warming the family and providing the heat necessary to cook meals.

And then there's the quiet. No hum of electricity mars the serenity. No whir of kitchen appliances, no roar of power tools in the shop and barns, no blaring of television or radio shows, and no ringing of phones interrupts the silence throughout the farm. Instead, the quiet is filled with the soft sounds of people working and talking and singing; children playing; and farm animals clucking, neighing, and mooing.

We see the Amish as having healthy family and community relationships, and we admire the profound and abiding faith in God that seems to influence all aspects of their lives. We see their ordered existence and deep sense of belonging, their quiet and peaceable lives—and we yearn for these same things in our own families.

Most of us aren't prepared to "go Amish." We're not ready to give up cars, electricity, and technology to move onto a farm and live a plain life. But it doesn't have to be an all or nothing proposition. We can look to the Amish to discover qualities and ways of doing things that we can incorporate into our *Englisha* lives to help us slow down, live more simply, and enjoy the blessings God gives—all without leaving home.

The apostle Paul advises, "Make it your ambition to lead a quiet life and attend to your own business and work with your hands...so that you will behave properly toward outsiders and not be in any need" (1 Thessalonians 4:11-12 NASB). I believe that is what appeals to us about the Amish. We long to live quietly and peacefully with our friends and neighbors, take pleasure in work well done, care for those in our midst who are less fortunate or face unexpected crises, and serve the needs of our communities. And always with hearts and minds that pray, "Your will be done, Lord."

◆ ◆ ◆ ◆ ◆

The path of the righteous is like the morning sun,
shining ever brighter till the full light of day.

PROVERBS 4:18

1

Family First

◆ ◆

Children are a heritage from the LORD,
offspring a reward from him.

PSALM 127:3

For the Amish, the family is central to their way of life. Having many children is considered a blessing by God, and, as a result, large families are the norm. In fact, the Amish population is one of the fastest growing segments in North America today. It's estimated that 80 to 85 percent of children born to Amish parents remain Amish as adults. When a young couple marries, it's a given that their most important task is to raise a family in the admonition and nurture of the Lord and according to the rules of their Amish church district.

When a child is born into an Amish family, there is rejoicing. Friends and family soon come to meet the new little one, and they will often bring small gifts, such as food or some other practical item. When children are born with health or developmental issues, they are considered God's special ones and are cared for lovingly by their families. According to their abilities, the children are encouraged and taught to participate as much as possible in daily family and community life.

Babies and very young children are picked up and cuddled often, and there always seems to be someone around to keep them occupied and content. Unmarried aunts might help the new mother with the endless round of chores and projects that need attention, whether canning the hundreds of jars of food needed for the winter months, planting or weeding the garden, or cooking and baking for the family.

Older brothers and sisters include their younger siblings in work and play, teaching by doing. Mom and Dad are quick to show their children how to perform small jobs, and children soon learn that their help is appreciated. They are loved and needed members of the family. The Amish understand that good attitudes and good habits start at a tender age.

As children grow, they are given increasingly more responsibilities. At the age of three or four, a girl might be given the task of sweeping the kitchen floor or folding the towels. In another year or so, she could be responsible for collecting eggs from the henhouse and feeding and watering the family's small flock of chickens. If the father works at home, which is the ideal state of affairs for the Amish, a young boy will follow his father to the fields or the shop and work alongside him.

Discipline is thorough, and from an early age Amish children know what is expected of them. They learn to obey the authority of their parents, who in turn model obedience by conforming to the church *ordnung* (a set of rules that govern all aspects of Amish life in that particular community).

Amish children go to school through the eighth grade, typically in one- or two-room schoolhouses built and maintained by the community. The children are usually taught by a young, unmarried Amish woman, and when they graduate they are well prepared for living the Amish life. After graduation, youth spend their days working alongside parents or apprenticing with other Amish to learn trades sanctioned by their church district. Often they carry on small business endeavors, such as running a family produce stand, making and selling handcrafted items, or working in a bakery. They are allowed to keep some of their earnings, or they hand the entire amount over to their parents. The parents use the income to help support the family or put it away for when the children marry and set up their own housekeeping. Teens work hard, but they are also given freedom to spend time with other youth in their district and neighboring ones.

Beginning at about age 16, Amish youth begin *rumspringa*, a "running around" period that usually lasts until they choose to be baptized and join church. During these years, teens participate in singings and planned activities, such as ice skating in winter or corn husking bees in the fall. This period between childhood and adulthood is when Amish youth decide whether they will be baptized and fully commit to the Amish way of life or leave the community. When *rumspringing*, some Amish youth may wear *Englisha* clothing, cut their hair in *Englisha* fashion, and even drive cars. Parents and church leaders don't condone these practices, but they know becoming a baptized member of the Amish church is a lifelong decision that shouldn't be rushed or forced. This is also the time when dating and courtship often take place. Young adults usually begin baptismal classes once they've decided to marry.

Weddings traditionally take place in November and December, after the annual harvest is complete. These are festive-yet-serious occasions because the Amish believe marriage is for life. Divorce is not an option. The young couple is "published" during church several weeks prior to the big event, and preparations kick into high gear the week before the wedding. The house and outbuildings where the wedding is to take place are scrubbed clean. The guest list can exceed 300 people. A new "Sunday dress" is sewn for the bride-to-be and a shirt is made for the groom. Food is distributed to the many cooks who will help prepare dishes for the big day. Table servers are assigned for the meal, and personal attendants for the bride and groom are chosen.

The wedding day begins early and ends late. First there is the wedding service, which can last three or more hours. After that, the main meal is served. Visiting takes up much of the afternoon, and a "singing" for the youth takes place in the evening, along with another meal.

Parents help their married children as much as they are able, and they will often turn over the family farm or business to a married son or daughter for a reasonable price. Often a younger son will take over the family farm, and the parents will move into a *daadi haus* (grandparents' house) built for them on the farm property. The older generation will help when needed. This doesn't mean labor stops for the grandparents. Often they start a second season of work, perhaps opening a small repair shop or bulk-foods store or making small, wooden handcrafts or quilts to sell to tourists. In this way, they are gainfully occupied and yet have the opportunity to slow down a bit and not work as hard physically as they did in their earlier years. Furthermore, they are still on the family land, ready to lend a hand if the young family needs help.

The Amish way of life highlights the family. There is never a time when a person is considered a liability, no matter if young, old, infirm, or disabled in some way. Each person is loved, honored, and welcomed in the family circle.

◆ What the Amish Can Teach Us ◆

To Amish children, the family is the center of their universe, and it is within the family structure that they learn Amish values. Families eat together, pray together, worship together, sing together, and work together daily. Extended families visit back and forth, which further cements familial ties that bind. The Amish know they can count on their families to support and help them during difficult times.

Practicing this "family first" attitude will help us strengthen our ties to each other. In today's world, we've lost much of that understanding. The family is no longer a cohesive unit where members are confident they are loved and supported. So how can we reestablish the family as a central unit? How can we strengthen our families so each member feels loved, valued, and important? Let's look at some habits and patterns for daily living that we can use to help build up our families.

Helping Your Family Thrive

Children don't need the latest new gadget as much as they need loving parents who are mindfully there for them day in and day out. Children won't be able to develop a confident sense of belonging if their parents are always on the go. Just as the Amish keep their children close during the day because they believe it's best for a child's healthy emotional development, we can organize our schedules to include as much family time as possible.

Develop a vision for "family first." Decide what your priorities are for your family and live accordingly. Develop a family mission statement, and refer to it often to help you stay on track. You can become so busy making a living that you easily lose sight of the reasons why you are working so hard in the first place. These reminders will help your family grow close and flourish.

Many parents currently leave home each day to go to work to earn money to pay for necessities, such as food and shelter. For many, it's not possible for one or both parents to stay home with the children. I encourage you to carefully think through just how much income you need as a family. Develop a budget, and then decide what you can do without. I'm not advocating an austerity program, but you may be surprised to find areas where you can simplify and make do, thus reducing your monthly outlay. And with that reduced monthly budget, you may be able to work less and stay home more. Everyone wins.

Another important area often undervalued is making your home safe, clean, and orderly. Children thrive on routine (and so do their parents), so make it a practice to have daily and weekly cleaning schedules that everyone can count on and work toward. Another good practice is to have the family spend a few minutes each evening picking up items used during the day. Put away papers and toys and straighten up a bit. Waking up to a neat home starts the day off right.

Family Fun Night

Have a regular family fun night. Plan to spend the evening together as a family doing something enjoyable. For instance, you could study something the whole family can take an interest in. These evening activities can be simple, but it's also fun to occasionally plan ahead for something a bit more involved. Would you like some suggestions for family night? Here are 50 ideas to get you started.

- Bird watch. A good set of binoculars and a bird identification book for your area will help enormously.

- Take a walk in the park or hike on a nature trail.

- Memorize Bible verses together.

- Ride bikes.

- Visit the library.

- Enjoy a backyard cookout.

- Make s'mores around a backyard BBQ or fireplace and sing campfire songs.

- Pick a book to read aloud together. Read a chapter or two each evening.

- Fly kites.

- Have a "help others night." Encourage everyone to go through closets and toy boxes. Fill up a giveaway bag and take it to an organization that sells used goods at bargain prices to people who are struggling to get by. Go together as a family to drop off the items, and then celebrate with ice-cream cones.

- Have a family potluck night. Each person makes something for dinner. Even toddlers can join in by opening a package of crackers or setting out bread and butter.

- Dream up a theme for the day or evening, such as Old West Night. Have everyone dress up in cowboy/cowgirl clothes, cook up some grub, such as beans and cornbread, and rent a Western movie.

- Put on a special music night. You can make your own instruments or use instruments you have, write your own songs or use ones everyone knows, or even sing a cappella. Then put on a concert.

- Tape butcher paper to an outside house or garage wall and

paint a mural. For easy cleanup, use washable paints if your children are young.

- Hold an art appreciation evening. Get some books from the library, and learn about different schools of art. Choose your favorites.
- Bake cookies and take them to neighbors.
- Make pizzas. For easy preparation, use English muffins for the crust.
- Put together a family soup meal. Everyone gets to choose one ingredient to add to the pot.
- If the weather is warm, have an outdoor water fight. You can use water balloons or squirt guns.
- Make your own sundaes. Have plenty of goodies to sprinkle on top.
- Meet "under the big tent." Drape a sheet over your kitchen table or use chair backs to hold up a sheet. Spend the evening under the tent eating dinner, playing games, and reading together. Use flashlights for even more fun.
- Play group games.
- Enjoy a classic movie.
- Put on a talent show and invite friends.
- Learn to dance or have fun doing your own dance thing. Play different styles of music and dance the way the music makes you feel.
- Host a formal evening. Make a special dinner, dress up in party clothes, light candles, use the good china.
- Make birdhouses or bird feeders and put them in the yard.
- Write letters to grandparents or loved ones.
- Write letters of appreciation to your pastor.

- Make a family flowerpot. Each person gets to choose one annual flowering plant to put in a large pot. Place the pot near the door so every time family members enter or exit the house they see the bright flowers and are reminded that family belongs together. This is great to do around Mother's Day.

- Stargaze.

- Enjoy a family campout. Spend the night outside "roughing it" in the wilds or in your backyard.

- Make a home movie.

- As a family, write and illustrate a story.

- Volunteer to clean the home or yard of someone who is laid up or elderly. Then work together as a family to get the job done.

- Go to a secondhand store and find fun clothing and accessories to make costumes. Then have a costume party.

- Create a family newsletter, and send it to all your relatives.

- Hold a show-and-tell. Everyone gets to talk about something that's special to him or her.

- As a family, volunteer to clean the church or work on a mission project.

- Eat with your fingers. Consume an entire meal without using silverware.

- Pretend you're pioneers. What would pioneers be doing?

- Hold a family slumber party in the living room.

- Go through your photos and talk about family history.

- Rake autumn leaves into a gigantic pile and take turns jumping into it.

- Grab some magnifying glasses and go on a backyard bug safari.

- Dig for buried treasure. (Mom and Dad can bury "treasures" in clean sandboxes or garden areas.)

- Go to an animal shelter to pet the cats and take some dogs for a walk.

- Hold a "turn the tables" night. Let the kids be in charge of the meal and the evening. Help them shop for groceries if needed. Let them choose and lead the evening's entertainment.

- Go on a treasure hunt. Write out clues that lead to other clues. Send participants all over the house and yard in search of treasure you've hidden.

- Make homemade calendars for grandparents. Draw pictures and write inspirational verses on the pages.

Some activities will work so well that your family will want to do them again and again. That's great. The idea is to have regular, fun family time together.

Parents as Teachers

When my sons were young, I always said my hope was to parent my way right out of the job. In other words, I wanted my boys to grow up to be responsible adults who were able to take care of themselves and, if God ordained, their wives and children. That is a commendable goal for all parents, and one the Amish seem to achieve. They include their children in all aspects of life from an early age. When the children leave school for good after the eighth grade, they begin working alongside their parents. In this way, they are maturing into adult roles.

You too can diligently teach your children and help them mature into responsible, industrious, and well-balanced individuals. You can help them with their homework and project assignments, teach them how to clean and maintain the house and yard, and when they're old enough, show them how to balance a checkbook and set a budget. Let them be responsible for the family's meals once or twice a week (you can help them plan and shop for groceries if needed). Teach them routine vehicle maintenance, such as when to get the oil changed and how to put air in the tires. Think about what they'll need to know when they leave home, and make sure they have a good foundation for success in those areas.

Establish Family Traditions

Holidays are especially good times to establish family traditions, such as holding a family decorate-for-Christmas evening. But you don't have to be limited to special times. Any positive thing repeated can become a good family tradition. It can be something as simple as an encouraging cheer used when someone in the family has a big day ahead of them. Or it could be something a bit more elaborate, such as having special themes for birthday celebrations.

Our family has several traditions that take place on Thanksgiving. One tradition is that I roast a turkey with all the trimmings. The dinner menu doesn't change much from year to year, and we all eat way more than is good for us. Every year we begin this feast of overabundance the same way. I place five kernels of corn on each plate, and then remind the family that five kernels of corn were supposedly the daily ration for the Pilgrims during the terrible winter prior to the first harvest. Although I've heard this is true, even if it's not historically accurate, this tradition is a good visual reminder of how much we have to be thankful for.

Working Together

Finding meaningful work to undertake as a family gives rewards far in excess of a job simply ticked off the family's to-do list. When a family works together, youngsters learn how to work as members of a team instead of as competitors. They discover they can count on others to perform their assigned tasks just as they are being counted on to perform their parts. They learn good communication skills—listening and speaking. They gain proficiency in conveying what they mean and deciphering instructions from others. They'll realize that each person has talents, and that taken as a whole, a project is far more likely to succeed than if they tried to accomplish it on their own. Children also learn that working together makes the time pass more pleasantly and that a difficult or tedious task isn't quite so onerous when shared.

Celebrate Special Moments

There are so many reasons to celebrate your family. Remembering to do so is often simply a matter of becoming attuned to those reasons. And there's no need to have to plan and execute an elaborate event. Simple actions, such as a special plate at the dinner table or a handwritten note from other family members, touch the heart. Keeping things low-key makes it easier to encourage an attitude of celebration. In many instances, it really is the thought that counts. And the reason for celebrating doesn't have to be for something spectacular or impressive. Celebrate the small joys in life also. Here are a few good reasons to celebrate that may help get your own ideas flowing.

- birthdays and holidays
- well-earned grade at school (even if it's not an A)
- "firsts" and "lasts," such as first lost tooth, last day of school, first time tying shoelaces, last time using a booster car seat
- getting "caught doing an act of kindness"
- a goal or achievement realized
- first day of spring, summer, fall, or winter
- return of the swallows (or any animals your family enjoys)
- winning a game or losing a game with grace
- a full moon
- just because

Family Times Are Fleeting

When all is said and done, your kids won't remember how many raises or promotions you got. What they *will* remember are the many times spent together as a family, whether it's doing something fun or just hanging out. They'll remember some of the valuable lessons you imparted, as well as the funny moments that will be told over and over again. Spending time together as a family is one of the best gifts you can give your kids.

I realize when babies and toddlers are in the house, the days and weeks sometime seem to drag. The endless rounds of feeding, changing diapers, and cleaning up messes stretch out before us. But seasoned parents will tell you it seems like only yesterday that their children were helpless little ones and today they are adults embarking on their own paths. So despite the nights of interrupted sleep and the never-ending work of maintaining a home, I encourage you to spend time together as a family. The bonds and supportive atmosphere you nurture will impact their entire lives...and yours! Start making precious memories today. And when your kids grow up and move out, they'll eventually realize that Mom and Dad really did know what they were talking about all those years. And because of the time you spent together as a family, your children will always know they can come to you and trust your input. They'll never be too old to ask for your perspective on thorny issues or ask for your advice.

Now that's a job well done!

2

Building Community

◆◆◆◆◆◆◆◆◆◆◆◆◆◆◆◆◆◆◆◆◆◆◆◆◆◆◆◆

*They were continually devoting themselves to the apostles' teaching
and to fellowship, to the breaking of bread and to prayer.*

ACTS 2:42 NASB

We've all seen the compelling images of an Amish barn raising. Do you wish you could experience such a day? Do you think of the pleasure and satisfaction that might come from work frolics, silo-fillings, and husking bees, where family and friends pitch in to get a big job done? And then there are the ubiquitous *grossdaadi häuser* in Amish country. They are the homes the older generations move into located on family farms and close to the rhythms of daily life. Fellowship time and church services on Sunday are more meaningful when we're surrounded by loved ones and close friends.

We tend to view the Amish with a sense of nostalgia because their communities remind us of simpler, gentler times in history, when families stuck together and neighbors pitched in to help each other out. In rural settings, people pretty much knew everyone in their community. Even if they weren't close friends with someone, they certainly knew something about the person's family history. Life happened on a human scale, and what a person did was noticed. Even today, we aren't many generations past this largely agrarian, small-scale lifestyle, so we sometimes wish we could go back to those good old days. And yet this desire for community extends even further back—all the way back to the Garden of Eden and how God made us.

When God placed Adam in the Garden of Eden, Adam felt a lack even though he was surrounded by all the plants and animals in that beautiful place. He was lonely, so God supplied Eve to meet his need. Adam was so pleased with God's gift that he joyously cried out, "This is now bone of my bones and flesh of my flesh" (Genesis 2:23). Since that time, things haven't really changed. We all thrive on knowing and being known by others. Because we live in a fallen world, it's no longer a perfect system, but our desire for community remains. All of us—including the Amish—place great store in our relationships with others.

For the Amish, community is everywhere—in their church traditions, family relationships, friendships, and business dealings. They often have lifelong friendships, and marriage vows are taken until death do them part. They believe Jesus Christ is their Savior, and that He is also their greatest teacher for how to live godly lives. Because of this, the Amish promote a servant's attitude. They use the word "JOY" to explain this attitude: *J* is for *Jesus*—He is first; *O* is for *others*—they come next; *Y* is for *you*—you are last. This is just one helpful reminder that showing kindness and generosity to others is what is expected throughout life.

Church services are another way the Amish strengthen community ties. Church is held every other Sunday, although in most districts there are no church buildings. Instead, the Amish meet in one another's homes. The hosting family provides a meal afterward, and visiting takes place before the families leave for home and evening chores.

Twice each year, a communion service takes place, but only if all church members are in agreement in all matters. If there are any divisive issues, communion will be put off until such time as harmony among the parties is restored, so it becomes necessary to figure out ways to get along with one another for the sake of group unity.

Dying to self or denying self-will is a strong directive in Amish culture that also helps strengthen the ties that bind. From an early age, children learn what it means to submit to the group dynamics and to the authority placed over them in the form of parents, teachers, older siblings, other relatives, and church officials. The Amish find this attitude of submission modeled in Christ Jesus, who, though born a king, humbled Himself even to death on a cross for us. This ultimate act of God's will—not self-will—is the standard by which the Amish strive to live. As a result, they are quick to lend a helping hand whenever a need within the community arises, and they pitch in with a willing attitude when there is work to be done.

Strong community also shows up in other ways. Visiting on off-church Sundays takes priority for many families, as well as visits to shut-ins, the elderly, and those who are ill or injured. Insurance is almost never bought because church members help each other out in times of need. Business transactions with other Amish take precedence over buying from outsiders.

And then there are the Amish parochial schools—one or two classrooms contain all eight grades. There is Bible reading and a hymn is sung every morning, which help to strengthen community identity and a person's place within that community. The curriculum used stresses practical basics, and Amish students are expected to thoroughly learn the subjects. Competition is downplayed. Older students assist younger students, and slow learners will get helped by quick learners, so every student successfully acquires the knowledge they will need as adults in the community.

Many Amish speak a German dialect among themselves, so the children often don't learn English until they attend school. Speaking German as a group also adds to their tight sense of community. Their dialect is for insiders only, although the Amish would never characterize it as such.

◆ WHAT THE AMISH CAN TEACH US ◆

The Amish are fortunate in that their community overlaps. They attend church with the same people they go to school with and work with, for the most part. This enables them to develop deep, meaningful relationships with the people around them. Further, the Amish are visibly set apart because of their distinctive dress, so they can easily tell if a stranger is among them.

Our communities aren't as clear cut. We might be members of several communities or groups of people. The people we work with might not be the same people who attend our church, and the people who live close to us might not be the same people we went to school with. But this doesn't have to hinder us from developing strong relationships and forming groups of people who care for one another. Let's explore some ways we can build a sense of community.

A Family Day of Rest

The idea that Sundays are a day of rest and restoration seems to be an antiquated notion these days. But I have fond memories of just those kinds of times. Back when I was a child, stores and gas stations were closed and commerce stopped on Sundays. Today it's hard to imagine not being able to go out and get a gallon of milk or fill your vehicle with gas on any day at any time. On Sundays back in the old days, you'd have to wait until Monday when the stores opened. People had to plan ahead.

When I was a child, we prepared for Sunday. We all took showers on Saturday night, and Mama would sometimes tie rags in our hair to make curls for the morning. We'd set out our good clothes, and Mama or Dad would shine everyone's shoes so we'd look our best for church. (Oh how I loved those shiny shoes! We only got two pairs of shoes a year, and having them freshly polished was almost as good as having a new pair.) Sunday afternoons after church were spent reading books while our parents catnapped. Later we'd help Mama prepare Sunday dinner, which was always a bit more elaborate than usual. Although my mother always had the cookie jar full, Sunday was the only day of the week we had actual *dessert*—some kind of pie, cake, or pudding. I especially looked forward to that. We often had relatives in to share the meal with us. Those restful Sundays and special Sunday dinners were a great way to begin the new week—refreshed and ready to go.

The term "Sabbath" comes from the Hebrew verb *shabbat,* which means to "cease, end, or rest." In the Bible, we read that "by the seventh day God completed His work which He had done, and He rested on the seventh day from all His work which He had done. Then God blessed the seventh day and sanctified it, because in it He rested from all His work" (Genesis 2:2-3 NASB). How can we keep our Sabbath days restful?

- First, choose a day as your Sabbath. If possible, combine your Sabbath rest day with your church attendance day. This is such a perfect pairing because God is the One who taught us about resting.

- Prepare for your Sabbath day as much as possible during the week so you can keep work to a minimum on your chosen day of rest.

- Consider sharing part of your rest day with another like-minded family, perhaps enjoying a Bible study and sharing a meal.

- You can spend some time reading the Bible and praying or take a walk or sit outside to contemplate the beauty of God's creation.

- Unplug for the day. No television; no Internet. Yes, I realize this may seem impossible, but it can be done!

Connecting with People at Church

At first glance, feeling connected with people who attend the same church you do would seem easy to accomplish. You are, after all, with a group of like-minded folks, so fitting in and being comfortable should be simple. But reality can be far different. And if you sometimes feel separate, others probably do too.

The Amish don't struggle with this as much as we do because they're required to go to the church nearest to where they live. We, on the other hand, can church hop with impunity, making it difficult to settle down and become attached to and involved in one church body. But there are lasting benefits when we consider our church family just as it implies—as family. And just as in real families, there will sometimes be hard feelings and disagreements to work through. But also like healthy families, there will be many more moments of joy and peace that come from intimately knowing others and loving them over a long period of time.

If your desire is to get involved with your church and help build community there, here are some practical ideas to use as a jumping-off point.

- Participate in church activities in addition to attending church on Sundays. Attend Sunday school, a midweek service, or a prayer breakfast, for example.

- Start a new church activity or ministry.

- Each week learn the name of one person you don't know well yet. Spend time getting to know a bit about him or her. Say hello, using his or her first name each time you see the person.

- If your church keeps a birthday calendar, send a card or short note recognizing each member on his or her special day.

- Start a multigenerational home group that meets once a month for an afternoon or evening of fun and sharing. Enjoy a potluck meal together.

- Design and coordinate a church community garden. Share the harvest with the entire church family or donate the produce to an organization that feeds the hungry and homeless.

- Organize "card showers," where people send encouraging cards to shut-ins, the elderly, people who are sick or injured, and people who are struggling.

- Make a sunshine box for a family or individual who could use a bit of cheer and encouragement. Sunshine boxes

consist of small wrapped gifts with a card that explains
the recipient is to open one a day. Get creative! These gifts
don't have to cost money.

- Invite people to your home for a meal or dessert.

- Get to know the people you attend church with outside
of church. Meet up in a park to have some playtime, walk
together on a nearby nature trail, or take a leisurely bike
ride together.

- Pray regularly for members of your church and for the pas-
tors and teachers.

Building Community in Your Neighborhood

I raised my family in the country, but now that my boys are grown
and have families of their own, I decided to downsize. Several years
ago I moved into a small town, so now I'm surrounded by close neighbors. I've found that it was easier getting to know my country neighbors than it was getting to know the people who live within a stone's
throw of my house.

When we moved to our place in the country, we couldn't see another
house from our property, and the narrow lane we lived on only had
two other homes tucked away further up. But the neighbors knew
there were new folks moving in, and within two days several from the
surrounding area had dropped in to bring treats, a meal, or simply to
introduce themselves.

These introductions were the beginning of some good friendships,
and I knew I could count on my neighbors in a pinch. For several
years we had an annual neighborhood turkey butchering day. One
self-described "Oklahoma hog farmer" taught us everything we could
ever want to know about raising tender, tasty pork by using a mash barrel. Plant starts were regularly passed back and forth, and I rarely came
home from a visit without a small gift or food item being pressed into
my hand upon leaving.

When I moved to my town neighborhood, I was a bit surprised

when no one came over to introduce themselves. I got a few waves and smiles from a distance, but my new neighbors seemed reticent to come over and start a conversation. *Odd,* I thought, so I decided to help things along.

I keep a stash of inexpensive pie plates so when I make pies for people and they forget to return the plates, I always have some on hand. Since I'd moved in during the month of October, I decided pumpkin pies were just the thing for breaking the ice. I made a pie for each of my near neighbors and hand-delivered them so I could introduce myself. It worked like a charm.

Today one neighbor and I love to discuss our vegetable gardens and canning projects. (He's a single dad raising his teenage daughter alone.) Another neighbor shares his ongoing medical issues, which are difficult for him to bear gracefully at times because there is no cure for what ails him. Yet another neighbor, a very sweet girl who favors black clothing and has piercings and tattoos, is my walking buddy. Slowly I'm learning about their lives, and even though they aren't Christians, they are aware that I am. So when I say I'll pray about something, they know I will. And when I follow up and ask how things are going, they don't turn away or close off. They accept me just as I accept them.

Yes, there may be times when nothing you do can bridge the gap between you and a neighbor. In that case, simply smile and wave when you meet, and try to be the best neighbor *you* can be.

As I've noted, we can get so busy with life that we easily forgo friendships with our neighbors because, aside from sharing a neighborhood, we might not have much in common. But I've learned since moving to town that people usually have much more in common than first meets the eye. I've enjoyed getting to know the wonderful people who live near me, and I encourage you to do the same with your neighbors. How can you do that?

- Make some treats or other small homemade gifts. Take them to your neighbors and introduce yourself.

- Plan a neighborhood movie night. Use a smooth wall or

garage door or put up a white sheet. Rent a family friendly movie and pop lots of popcorn.

- Make a "trading post" and place it in your front yard. Any container that keeps out the weather will do. If you use a large box, the kids will love decorating it. If someone in your family has carpentry skills, by all means have him or her build a simple structure that looks like an old-time, miniature trading post building. Locate it where you can secure it to a post or fence. Make sure the "counter" is low enough that even the younger kids can see inside. Place small objects, such as used books, dollar-store goodies, or humorous stories and jokes inside, and let people take out what they want. Encourage neighbors to replace what they take with an item so the trading post will remain stocked.

- Invite your neighbors to a meteor shower viewing. The Perseid meteor showers usually peak between August 9 and August 14 in the continental United States, with as many as 60 meteors per hour. The later in the evening you watch, the better your chances of seeing them. Unless there is cloud cover or the lights in your city are fierce, you shouldn't get skunked.

- Host a holiday party. On the Fourth of July you could hold a bike parade. On Easter, you could facilitate an Easter egg hunt.

- Organize a neighborhood spring yard cleanup. Plant some pretty annuals to brighten the neighborhood while you're at it.

- Barter with a neighbor for help with a project you can't accomplish on your own.

- Create a quarterly community newsletter. Use the space for news that affects your neighborhood and introduce new families who have recently moved in.

- Place a portable fire pit in your front yard, and invite the neighbors to join you for a fireside visit.

- Hold an ice-cream social.

- Attend town meetings to stay abreast of changes in regulations, and then share the news with your neighbors.

- Host a neighborhood meeting, and invite local law enforcement to come to speak on safety issues.

- Take new neighbors a tasty meal. Include the recipe for a nice added touch.

- Offer to rake leaves, weed, or shovel snow for an elderly or disabled neighbor.

- If you garden, distribute any excess harvest to your neighbors who don't garden.

- Plant a community garden, large or small.

- Ask a neighbor to join you for exercise or walking on a regular basis.

- Have a chili (or other food item) cook-off.

- If your budget allows, hire neighborhood teens to do odd jobs for you.

- Organize a neighborhood-wide garage sale.

- Request favorite recipes from each household and put together a neighborhood cookbook. Give everyone a copy.

The expression "good fences make good neighbors" may be true in certain situations, but I think this is a better expression: "Good neighbors make good neighbors." Do your best to be the kind of neighbor you would like to have. Always pray for your neighbors and neighborhood. It can make all the difference!

3

Housekeeping Tips

◆ ◆

Unless the LORD *builds the house, they labor in vain who build it.*

PSALM 127:1 NASB

Amish women are known to be frugal, and many run their homes using old-fashioned methods and tools. Travel through an Amish community, and you're liable to see laundry on clotheslines, large vegetable and flower gardens, and orchards, grape arbors, or berry vines tucked away around back. Because most districts don't use highline electricity, alternative energy sources and lower consumption are common. And if you're fortunate enough to be invited into an Amish home, you'll notice right away that they tend toward simplicity in their furnishings. Their homes are spotless and well organized. They daily live the adage, "A place for everything, and everything in its place."

Amish women are industrious, and they can get more accomplished in a single day than many people care to tackle in a week's time. And Amish women do this amount of work day in and day out with precious few time- or labor-saving devices, such as vacuums, dishwashers, clothes dryers, and bread machines.

Let's say an Amish family has seven children. This means that every day this Amish wife and mother will need to prepare enough food to fill 27 hungry appetites (over the course of three meals). Unless she has daughters old enough to help, this wife will hand wash and dry 27 plates, 27 glasses, 81 pieces of silverware, plus numerous cooking and serving utensils, and the many platters, bowls, pots, and pans that were dirtied as she prepared and served all that food. And since Amish families enjoy bread and dessert at every meal, our Amish wife will need to keep up with the daily demand for bread, pies, cookies, cakes, biscuits, rolls, and other goodies—and do all the dishes related to making those. All this amounts to a lot of time spent in the kitchen every day. But that's only a part of what occupies her.

Once or twice a week there's the laundry to attend to. With nine people in the family, that's a staggering amount of clothing, towels, and sheets to keep clean. On laundry day, heaps of water must be heated and then hauled to the washing machine, which may or may not have a gasoline engine to agitate the load. Next, the laundry must be rinsed in clean water (more water hauling) and then rolled through a ringer to squeeze as much of the water out as possible. After that, the heavy, wet loads are carried to the clothesline and hung to dry. Once the clothes are dry, it's time to heat the irons on the woodstove and press everything neatly.

The floors must be scrubbed, the beds made, and the living areas tidied and dusted. Windows and walls need to be washed and the porches swept. Sewing and mending for all the family members seem to be never-ending tasks. Outside, there's lawn mowing and planting and weeding to be done. Chickens must be watered and fed and fresh eggs gathered. In season, the family garden must be harvested, and hundreds of jars of food need to be preserved for the coming winter. Making quilts to sell or working in a cottage industry on the property can also take up hours in her day.

The list of tasks is long, but the Amish know how to work. In fact, their industriousness is one of the stumbling blocks for people seeking to join their communities. If people haven't been taught to work hard when they're young, it's difficult to catch that work ethic later in life. For the Amish, working hard is embraced as part of what it means to be an adult. And because their work serves the purpose of caring for those they love, its considered a joy by most of them.

◆ WHAT THE AMISH CAN TEACH US ◆

Something that seems to be true for many Amish currently is they're one of the groups leading the way to living a sustainable lifestyle (although they would shun that notion). They make do with what they have, produce much of their own food, dress simply, wear out their clothes instead of having closets full of the latest fashions, use minimal electricity and gasoline, and repurpose, reuse, and recycle—just to name a few of their environmentally friendly lifestyle choices.

As I thought about Amish women and their housekeeping, the word *frugal* kept coming to my mind. Amish women don't spend their time shopping for the latest gadget guaranteed to make their lives easier. They don't buy the "new and improved" cleanser that promises to clean your house while you wait. Instead, they are at home caring for their families and, perhaps, using a bit more elbow grease than their *Englisha* counterparts. So toward that end, I want to share with you some down-home ideas and old-fashioned recipes for keeping your house clean and your family well cared for. These are great concoctions whether your home is in the country, in the city, or somewhere in between.

As we pick up new habits for living simply and choosing to tread a bit more lightly in certain areas, we find there is much we can discover from the Amish. Whether you try a few or all of these ideas, I'm sure you'll find some that grab your interest.

Organizing and Staying on Top of the Mess

There are entire books written on how to get organized in your home, and if that idea appeals to you, here are some good books that can help you get started:

- *More Hours in My Day* by Emilie Barnes and Sheri Torelli. This is one of the classic books on home management. You'll learn how to establish a simple organizational system that will save you time and money and free you from the unwanted stress that comes from being disorganized.

- *The House That Cleans Itself* by Mindy Starns Clark.
  Mindy uses a method she calls "horizontal thinking" that
  allows you to efficiently organize your home based on your
  particular household requirements. Mindy says this book
  is for the housekeeping impaired—and she's right!
- *Sidetracked Home Executives* by Pam Young and Peggy
  Jones. This book, written by two sisters, has been around
  for more than 30 years. It teaches how to organize your
  daily, weekly, and long-term housekeeping chores using a
  system of 3 x 5 cards. If you love keeping lists, you'll love
  this system.

If reading a book to learn how to whip your home into shape
doesn't sound like something you'd enjoy, here are some quick and
easy ideas to at least get you headed in the right direction. Very few of
us consider our homes in perfect order, and most of us agree we have
room for improvement in this area. So instead of fretting about how
far you are from that well-organized and clean home of your dreams,
pick an idea or two from the following list and just get going. You'll
be glad you did.

- *Stay on top of the dishes.* Make doing the dishes and cleaning the kitchen part of every mealtime. There's little
  that's more disheartening than dirty dishes cluttering
  up your sink and countertops when it's time to cook the
  next meal.
- *Sweep or vacuum high-traffic areas daily* (in my house that's
  the eat-in kitchen and the bathroom). Pick one other light-
  traffic area each day to vacuum or sweep, such as a bed-
  room or hallway. That way you'll get to all the floors in a
  week's time.
- *Get your most odious chore out of the way first.* That way it
  won't be hanging over your head throughout the day. And
  if you're a list maker, there is great satisfaction in ticking off

that particular job on the day's chore list. Everything else suddenly seems more doable because you've taken care of the headache job right up front.

- *Get up a bit earlier and knock off one or two items from your day's chore list before you head off to work.* It's satisfying to realize that it might only be eight o'clock in the morning but you've already accomplished something worthwhile.

- *Learn your daily energy rhythms and work with them.* I'm a morning person, and I love to hit the decks running so it's no problem for me to do some chores early, before I sit down to breakfast. But it's just as true that I start to run out of steam by noon. My sister-in-law, on the other hand, wakes up very slowly. She prefers to clean her house at night. When visiting her home, I've literally fallen asleep at night to the hum of the vacuum cleaner as my sister-in-law happily cleaned house.

- *Break down tasks into 10-minute increments.* Give yourself permission to take a break when those 10 minutes are up. Then go back at it again for another 10 minutes. Continue on until the task is done. For some of us, those 10 minutes may be the only real housework that gets done on some days. When I have one of those days, I remind myself that at least I'm 10 minutes closer to a clean house than I was before. I'm headed in the right direction.

- *Keep cleaning supplies and tools handy.* If you have to hunt through closets and cupboards to find what you need, chances are you won't get started. For years I used a heavy-duty plastic caddy with a sturdy handle to carry my cleaning supplies from room to room. Now I keep supplies in different parts of the house near where I use them. Both ways work. With the caddy, however, you only need to keep one of each item on hand, which might be more doable on a lean budget.

- *Choose a room a month to deep clean.* When my kids were young and interruptions were commonplace, I rarely cleaned an entire room in one session. Instead, I concentrated in spurts on a particular room for as long as it took me to really clean it top to bottom. Besides your daily cleaning routine, choose one room for the entire month to concentrate on. When you have spare moments during the month, work on that one room a bit at a time.

- Go through any closets and purge unused or unwanted items and organize what's left. Then go through drawers or cupboards and do the same thing. After eliminating unnecessary items, think "top to bottom." Take a dry mop to the corners up by the ceiling and sweep down any cobwebs. Then sweep down the walls, and wash any that have smudges or are dirty. After that wash the windows. Next comes dusting. If it warrants it, condition any wood. Then clean the floors, making sure to give special attention around the edges and in the corners.

- *Before bedtime, have everyone in the family straighten up the house.* If everybody pitches in, it takes only a few minutes to put away toys and projects and make sure everything is in order. Waking up to an orderly home makes for orderly living.

- *Don't let the mail pile up.* When you get the day's mail, go through everything and deal with it right away. Throw away junk mail and circulars instead of keeping them, thinking you'll get to them later. Have a designated spot to keep bills until it's time to pay them. Or consider going paperless and set up automatic payments.

- *Dig in and get the day's work done.* There's no substitute for simply taking charge. Dirt and clutter have a tendency to quickly get out of control, and the best remedy is to stay on top of things.

Having several good cleaning habits you incorporate daily into your household routine will go a long way toward maintaining a clean and orderly home.

Homemade Cleaners

Take a walk down the cleaning products aisle of any grocery store, and you'll immediately notice the smell. I always wondered about the chemicals used in those products that allowed the odors to permeate the packaging. If I stayed in that section for very long I'd sometimes get a headache. That bothered me, and when I became a mother I was even more concerned about what I was bringing into my home. Furthermore, when I thought about the cost of buying all those different products to clean my house, I knew there had to be a better way.

Being frugal by nature, I decided years ago that I would forgo these costly cleaners and use homemade products instead. I've been happily using low-cost, less-toxic cleaners with good results ever since. That's not to say I've never bought commercial cleaning products, because I have. But I love making and using homemade cleaners because I know what's in them. They are much, much less expensive than their store-bought counterparts. I'm also pleased to know my family is self-reliant in an increasingly consumer-driven world where even the most basic needs can't seem to be satisfied unless we go to the store and buy something.

If you decide to use some of my cleaning solutions, keep in mind that your results may vary. Exercise care and use sensible safety precautions when mixing and using these formulas. And remember to clearly mark the contents so if anyone comes across one of your containers, he or she will immediately know what's inside. This is especially important if you use recycled containers.

Vinegar

White distilled vinegar is probably my favorite all-purpose cleaner. I love the stuff, and I buy it by the gallon. I also appreciate the fact that vinegar is absolutely nontoxic so I never have to worry about little ones playing where I've recently cleaned. And it's cheap, which makes me even happier. An added bonus is that when I'm not using vinegar to clean something, I can use it to make a great salad dressing or perk up the flavor of cooked vegetables. What other cleaning product can boast that?

Here are some of the ways I use vinegar. (I know there are many more uses too.) These ideas will give you plenty of ways to use up a gallon in a hurry.

- *Mop the floors.* I add a good slug of vinegar—about one or two cups—to a sink full of warm water and mop my floors. The vinegar water cleans them well, and they dry with no streaking or soapy film left behind. I don't have to rinse either, which saves me a step. And once the floors are dry, there is no lingering vinegar smell.

- *Disinfect counters.* I regularly spray full-strength vinegar on my kitchen and bathroom counters and leave it there to air dry. Vinegar is a natural disinfectant, so it kills most bacteria, molds, and viruses. I always clean my kitchen counters this way before and after I process vegetables from my garden. That way I know I'm working on a clean surface, and I'm just as confident that my work area is clean once I've completed the task.

- *Clean and condition wood.* Mix a tablespoon of vinegar and a tablespoon of olive oil in a quart of warm water to clean and condition wood cabinets, furniture, and paneling on walls. I fill a quart jar and shake the contents well. Then I soak a rag (old, clean cloth diapers work great), wring it out really well, and wipe down the wood. If I'm feeling industrious, I follow with a dry-cloth wipe, but I've found that it's not necessary if I've wrung out the damp cloth well. Including the vinegar with the oil serves two purposes: the vinegar cleans and cuts grease and grime, and the oil seems to soak in better (as opposed to just sitting on the wood).

- *All-purpose cleaner/shiner.* For an all-purpose cleaner/shiner, I mix equal parts vinegar and water in a spray bottle. I use it to spray appliances, chrome cupboard and door handles, sink areas, and bathroom fixtures. I wipe things dry with a paper towel or rag. Sometimes I'll simply wet a rag instead of spraying directly on the surface of objects and go around and clean all the knobs in my house.

- *Clean windows and glass.* A quarter cup of vinegar mixed in a quart of water makes a great window and glass cleaner. I keep mine in a spray bottle, but you could just as easily use a bowl and dip a rag or sponge into the liquid and scrub away. I've always heard that using newspaper to clean and polish windows works best for a streak-free finish, but I personally dislike the way newspaper sounds when rubbing (it reminds me of fingers on a chalkboard), so I use paper towels or an old, clean diaper instead.

- *Eliminate mineral deposits.* Fill the reservoir of your automatic drip coffeemaker with vinegar. Let it sit for a half hour or so before you turn it on and let the vinegar run through the drip cycle. Repeat the drip cycle twice more using only water to thoroughly rinse away the vinegar. This will clean the hard water mineral deposits and make your coffee taste sweeter.

- *Clean the microwave.* In a four-cup, microwave-safe container (I use my four-cup glass measuring cup), mix together ½ cup vinegar and 1 ½ cups water. Place the container in your microwave oven, and microwave on high for about 2 minutes. Don't open the door, but let the vinegar mixture sit inside for 15 minutes or so. Remove the container and wipe down the microwave's interior walls with a damp cloth or sponge to remove the now-softened bits of food. This also deodorizes the interior.

- *In the dishwasher.* Pour half a cup or so of vinegar into the bottom of your automatic dishwasher, and run your dishes through as usual. The vinegar will help shine the glasses and get your dishes cleaner. It will also clean and deodorize your dishwasher and remove hard water stains from the interior.

- *Fruits and vegetables.* Use a tablespoon of vinegar for every cup of water to wash fruits and vegetables and kill any bacteria that might be present. Wash the produce with this mixture, and then rinse well with fresh water.

- *Washing clothes.* Use a cup of vinegar in the rinse cycle of your clothes washing machine. It will make your laundry soft and remove soap residue.

- *Disinfect baby toys.* To safely clean and disinfect baby toys (anything that is hard, such as plastic or wood), mix equal parts vinegar and water. If the toy can handle it, I immerse it in the solution for several minutes and then set it on a towel to dry. Otherwise, I use a wet rag to wipe it down.

- *Set and protect colors in material.* Have you ever made or bought something that has a rich color, such as bright red or deep purple, only to have the color bleed onto your other laundry? If I think I'm going to have a problem with the color bleeding, I immerse the fabric or wool in a bath of warm water and about a cup of vinegar. Then I rinse it with fresh water to see if the bleeding is still present. Sometimes I've had to do this two or three times before the color sets. And every once in a while it seems that no matter what I do the color still wants to bleed. Then I purpose to always wash that item separately (at least I'm forewarned and don't ruin an entire load of laundry).

- *Nontoxic drain cleaner.* As a nontoxic drain cleaner, vinegar and baking soda can't be beat. To keep your drains unclogged, pour half a cup of baking soda into your drain and then follow that with half a cup of vinegar. The resulting volcano is great entertainment. Let the mixture sit for about 15 minutes and then pour boiling water down the drain. Do this once each month and you'll be good to go. If you have a clogged drain, don't be tempted to use a commercial drain cleaner. Instead, put in the baking soda and vinegar, and let it sit. Then pour in the boiling water. Using a clean toilet plunger, plunge until the clog shifts and the water disappears effortlessly down the drain. A few times over the years, I've had to plunge twice, but this method hasn't failed me yet.

Baking Soda

Common kitchen baking soda has become popular for more than just baking in the last few years. I'm glad because it's nontoxic, cheap, a natural deodorizer, and a gentle abrasive. When I was growing up, our family occasionally used baking soda to brush our teeth when we ran out of toothpaste. When we had colds, Mama would have us gargle with a pinch of baking soda and salt dissolved in a teacup of warm water. This concoction soothed our sore throats and seemed to get rid of the cold. When Dad complained of a sour stomach, he'd mix up a batch of baking soda and water and drink it down. Very soon he'd be feeling like his old self again.

Now that I have a home of my own, I've found even more uses for baking soda. When the family goes camping, I take baking soda along. It can be used to wash hands, scrub pots and pans, act as a deodorant, used in lieu of toothpaste, works as a poultice for itchy skin or insect bites, and, in a pinch, makes a great fire extinguisher. Now that's a multipurpose product!

Baking Soda as a Deodorizer

- *Refrigerator.* Stick an open box of baking soda in the corner of your refrigerator. Change it out every three months. When I replace the refrigerator soda, I use the open box

I've been using for cooking and open a new one for cooking. I want to use the freshest baking soda in my baking.

- *Trash cans and laundry baskets.* Sprinkle some baking soda in the bottom of trash cans and laundry baskets to keep things smelling fresh.

- *Shoes and boots.* Sprinkle some baking soda in your work boots or tennis shoes at night to eliminate odors. Shake it out before wearing them the next day.

- *Carpets and rugs.* To freshen carpets and rugs, sprinkle baking soda over them and let sit for several hours or overnight. Vacuum as usual. An added bonus is that this will make your vacuum cleaner smell better too. When we had a dog, I used baking soda regularly to help control the dog smell on our carpets and in the vacuum cleaner.

- *Lunch buckets.* Place a bowl of baking soda inside lunch buckets at night to get rid of odors that seem to linger there, especially in warm months.

Baking Soda as a Mild Abrasive

- *Porcelain cleanser.* Use baking soda as a safe cleanser for your sinks, tubs, and showers. It may take more elbow grease than using commercial cleansers, but it works and really shines up porcelain. When used regularly, baking soda also makes a great toilet cleanser. Simply shake it on, let it sit for a minute, and then scrub with a toilet brush. I keep a stash of baking soda right next to my kitchen sink in one of those glass bottles used for pouring sugar so I can easily grab it to scour my sink or scrub baked-on food in pots and pans. As long as the baking soda stays dry, it pours out of the little hole just like sugar. I put a soda cracker in the jar to soak up any moisture and keep the soda from caking. This works great.

- *Refrigerator grime.* Sprinkle some baking soda on a wet sponge and scrub the grime that mysteriously builds up on the top of the refrigerator. Wipe it clean with a wet rag. I also use this to scrub the greasy grime that builds up on the hood above my stove.

- *Oven cleaner.* To clean the inside of your oven, make a thick paste using baking soda and water. Pat it on and leave it overnight. The next morning, use a scrubber sponge and rub off the loosened food particles. Rinse well.

- *Toothpaste.* To use as toothpaste, place a small amount of baking soda in the palm of your hand and dip the wet bristles of your toothbrush into it. Brush your teeth, dipping as needed. Rinse your mouth well. Baking soda is also a great mouthwash! Simply add baking soda to warm water, swish in your mouth, spit, and rinse.

- *Skin cleanser.* To use as a face and body scrub, mix three parts baking soda to one part water. The paste is gentle enough to use on your face to clean and exfoliate. It also makes a great hand scrub for gardeners or people who get ground-in dirt on their hands.

- *Septic tanks.* When we lived in the country and had a septic system, every week or two I'd flush a cup of baking soda down the drain to help maintain the pH level in the septic tank.

- *Plastic containers.* If you use plastic food storage containers, they sometimes get pitted and start to smell. When they need freshening, fill them with baking soda dissolved in warm water and let stand overnight.

- *Hairbrushes and combs.* To clean the body and hair oils from your hairbrushes and combs, clean the hair out of the bristles. Then, in a quart jar, mix 2 tablespoons of baking soda and warm water. Soak the hairbrush and comb overnight.

- *Grease fires.* You can put out a small grease fire on your stove or in your oven by throwing *handfuls* of baking soda at the base of the flame to smother it. I've never had to use this method, thankfully, but it's nice to know my baking soda is nearby should I ever need to. (*Warning:* Never pour water on a grease fire.)

Ammonia

Ammonia has been used in homes for many years. It's inexpensive and works well for certain types of cleaning. *Never* use ammonia with bleach or anything with chlorine listed as an ingredient. The combination of ammonia and chlorine produces a potentially deadly gas. It's also a good idea to use ammonia only in well-ventilated areas. Also, don't stick your nose directly over the jug of ammonia when pouring. That said, if you use common sense, ammonia is a great addition to your household arsenal of cleaning products.

- *Heavy-duty cleanser.* For a heavy-duty cleanser, mix 2 tablespoons ammonia, ½ cup rubbing alcohol, and enough water to fill a quart-sized spray bottle. This makes an excellent window cleaner. It also works well for cleaning spills and such on the floor.

- *Soap scum.* Mix a strong solution of two parts ammonia to one part water and use it to clean soap scum from tubs, showers, and sinks.

- *Jewelry.* Pour ammonia into a cup or small bowl and soak your gold jewelry and diamond rings overnight. Rinse them well and let dry. Your jewelry will sparkle like new.

Chlorine Bleach

Some folks do not use chlorine bleach because they believe it's bad for a person's health and the environment. If you decide to use bleach as part of your cleaning routine, here are some suggestions.

- *Food preparation surfaces.* For kitchen counters and cutting boards, mix 1 teaspoon bleach to 1 quart of water in a spray bottle. Spray the areas to be sanitized. Let air dry. No need to rinse.

- *Cleaning hard surfaces.* For cleaning bathroom sinks, toilets, tubs, and showers, mix 2 ½ teaspoons bleach to 1 quart of water in a spray bottle. Spray the areas to be sanitized. Let air dry or allow the bleach to sit on the surface for at least a minute before wiping dry.

Remember that bleach and ammonia together produce highly toxic vapors. Urine produces ammonia, so never use a bleach solution where urine is present (such as around a toilet) unless the area has been cleaned and rinsed thoroughly.

If you can't smell the bleach when you use the solution, it is no longer strong enough to work, so you'll need to make a new batch.

Hydrogen Peroxide

You can purchase 3-percent hydrogen peroxide solution in brown bottles from drugstores. The brown bottles are important because hydrogen peroxide breaks down when exposed to light and will no longer be effective. If you mix up a batch of hydrogen peroxide and water, make sure your spray bottle keeps the light at bay. The following tips apply to the 3-percent solution only. Do not use stronger versions of hydrogen peroxide.

- *In the laundry.* Use hydrogen peroxide full strength—about ¾ cup per load—in your laundry as a bleach substitute.

- *Superficial wounds.* Pour onto a scratch or cut and watch it bubble up. Don't dry off the area until the bubbling has stopped.

- *Mouthwash.* Use hydrogen peroxide straight or mixed in equal parts with water as a mouthwash. Gargle, spit, and rinse.

- *Sanitizer.* Mix hydrogen peroxide and water in equal parts and put in a spray bottle that keeps out light. Use in the bathroom to sanitize counters, toilets, sinks, tubs, and showers.

Laundry Soap

Making homemade laundry soap is becoming increasingly popular with good reason. Many people consider commercial laundry detergents environmentally expensive to manufacture and use, and people with sensitive skin often have allergic reactions to some common commercial ingredients. Making your own laundry soap is easy, inexpensive, and fun—good reasons to give it a try.

When my kids were growing up, we'd butcher a hog or two each year for meat, and I'd render out the lard for baking and soap making. Once I had clean lard, I'd make a batch of lye soap and set it aside to condition and harden. When it was soap, I'd grate some of it to use for washing laundry. I'd dissolve the grated soap flakes in hot water, add some washing soda or borax if I had it on hand, and wash clothes. It was fairly straightforward, and aside from the preliminary step of making the homemade soap, it was quick and easy to make. If you're so inclined, by all means use your homemade soap, but the following two recipes can be made using store-bought soap if desired.

A quick note: In both of these recipes, the bar soap must be finely grated. I use my micro plane grater (a grater specially made out of strong stainless steel with tiny holes for grating peel zest and hard Parmesan cheese).

◆ ◆ ◆ ◆

HOMEMADE LAUNDRY SOAP (VERSION 1)

1 bar Fels-Naptha laundry soap
½ cup borax
1 cup washing soda (this is caustic so handle with care)

Yield: 150 loads or more

Finely grate the Fels-Naptha soap. Mix the grated soap flakes with the borax and washing soda. Store in a quart canning jar or other container with a tight-fitting lid.

To use: Make sure the ingredients are still well mixed. (I usually give it a few shakes before I open the lid.) Measure out 4 teaspoons and place in a quart jar or container with a watertight lid. Fill the quart container with very hot water. (I use the hot water from my insta-hot unit in my sink, but your hottest tap water will do.) Stir or shake until dissolved. Let it sit for several hours or overnight; it will thicken and turn into very thick gel. If it's separated, shake or stir it vigorously until it's evenly thick. Use ¼ to ½ cup per load. A cup of vinegar in the rinse water will help the clothes release all the soap and make them soft, fluffy, and very clean.

This recipe is great if space is an issue because you only have a quart container of the powdered mix to store.

❖ ❖ ❖ ❖

HOMEMADE LAUNDRY SOAP (VERSION 2)

1 bar Ivory or Kirk's castile soap
6 cups water
½ cup washing soda (this is caustic so handle with care)
½ cup borax
1 quart very hot water
2-gallon bucket or container with lid
1 gallon + 6 cups water

Yield: 64 laundry loads

Finely grate the bar of soap into a saucepan. Add 6 cups of water and heat on low until the soap flakes are melted. Slowly pour in the washing soda and borax, stirring constantly. Stir until powders are dissolved. You'll notice the washing soda wants to clump up, but keep stirring and smashing the big pieces, and eventually the liquid will clear and the powders will be completely dissolved. This takes around 5 minutes. Remove from heat.

Pour a quart of very hot water into the two-gallon bucket. Add the soap mixture and stir. Add 1 gallon plus 6 cups of water and stir again. Put the lid on and let the mixture sit for 24 hours to thicken.

To use: Stir the container if needed to evenly mix the ingredients. Measure out ½ cup of laundry soap gel per load. Adding a cup of vinegar during the rinse cycle will help to release the soap residue and make the clothes soft and clean.

This second recipe cleans about 64 loads of laundry and launders your clothes for just a few pennies per load.

◆ ◆ ◆ ◆

Washing Woolens and Delicates

Several years ago I happily discovered Orvus Paste horse shampoo. I'm a spinner and knitter, so I began using Orvus Paste to wash sheep fleece before processing the fiber. I was amazed at how clean they got. As a result of my knitting habit, my family has an inordinate number of woolens that must be washed by hand. We started using this shampoo to wash wool sweaters, socks, hats, and mittens. Then I read that Orvus Paste is also great for washing delicate fabrics, so I tried it on a very old lace doily that had a stain I couldn't get out, and it worked like a charm. I now use this shampoo for all my clothes that need to be hand washed.

I get Orvus Paste shampoo in a gallon jug from a local feed and farm store, but it comes in smaller containers also. The last gallon I bought was less than 20 dollars, and it will last me several years at least. For a slightly higher price per ounce, you can buy a smaller amount of Orvus Paste from some quilt shops, where it's sold as quilt soap. The shampoo is a thick sludge, except during hot weather when it might liquefy. No matter what the consistency, it works the same.

To hand wash woolens or other items, such as table linens and lace, I dip a large spoon into the jug to coat the spoon with the paste. Then I swish the spoon in a sink as I'm filling it with warm water (you can use hot or cold water, but I prefer a bit of heat because the shampoo dissolves better in warm water). Add the clothes item and let soak for about 15 minutes. After a good soaking, I gently wash the item, and then I lift it out of the water and drain. I refill the sink with clean water and rinse, and then repeat that step.

Soap for the Kitchen

During the time I attended a plain Mennonite church, I visited an older widow in her home. As we visited and hand washed the lunch dishes, I asked about the soap we were using. She informed me that it was homemade lye soap and water. *Well,* I thought, *I can do that.* So I went home and grated up some of my homemade soap into a container. I added boiling water and whisked until the soap was melted. I had homemade dish soap!

Unlike commercial kinds of soap, the following recipes for hand washing dishes won't make suds because they don't have a lot of additives. Contrary to what the ads for popular commercial dish soaps tout, the suds *are not* what cleans the dishes.

◆ ◆ ◆ ◆

ECONOMICAL LIQUID DISH SOAP

1 bar Ivory soap
8 cups very hot water

Finely grate the bar of soap. Add the hot water and whisk until the soap is melted. That's it! (Feel free to cut the recipe in half. Making a quart at a time is more manageable for my needs.)

This recipe is rock-bottom cheap, but sometimes when it sets up it's too thick to use in a pump-action soap dispenser. I store mine in a wide-mouthed, quart canning jar with a plastic lid. (A plastic container would work just as well and wouldn't be breakable.) I scoop out a few spoonfuls when I'm doing dishes or just pour a "glug" into the sink while I'm filling it with water. Depending on how it has thickened, I might add more water and stir to make sure it's all dissolved. Even though it's quite thick, I am usually still able to use a pump dispenser, so sometimes I do that.

Another bonus is this soap is also good as hand soap! That way I only have one container by my kitchen sink instead of two.

LIQUID DISH SOAP

½ cup liquid castile soap (such as Dr. Bronner's pure castile soap) *or* 1 T. (heaping) grated bar soap (Ivory or Kirk's castile soap)
1 ½ cups very hot water
1 T. white vinegar
1 T. washing soda

Mix all ingredients together and stir until the soap and soda have dissolved. Let cool on the counter, stirring occasionally.

If you use the grated bar soap, this recipe is still very inexpensive to make and use. Liquid castile soap tends to be expensive, so I don't use it often. Some nicely scented Dr. Bronner's castile soap might work better for you. This soap recipe doesn't get quite as thick as the Economical Liquid Dish Soap. Try both versions to see which one you prefer.

In the old days I didn't have an automatic dishwasher, but I do now. I've experimented with homemade dish soap to use in my automatic dishwasher. The following recipe worked great. Like the regular soap for washing dishes, it won't create suds because it doesn't have a lot of additives. Again, it's not the suds that get the dishes clean.

AUTOMATIC DISHWASHER SOAP

1 cup borax
1 cup washing soda or baking soda

¼ cup citric acid
¼ cup coarse kosher salt

Mix ingredients together. Use 1 tablespoon or so per dishwasher load. It's a good idea to add vinegar in the rinse container so the dishes will come out sparkling clean.

You can purchase citric acid at most grocery stores in the canning section. Sometimes stores only carry it during the summer months, so plan ahead if necessary. Citric acid helps get the soap residue off the dishes.

Borax is a disinfectant and deodorizer.

The kosher salt helps the soap do its job if you have hard water.

◆ ◆ ◆ ◆

Personal Care Products

Several years ago I taught a class at our local library. My plan was to have the class make body lotion and lip balm. I planned on 10 people signing up, based on the average number of attendees at these types of events. The results far exceeded my expectations, and I had to cut off the sign-ups at 25 people. I learned something very valuable: People are intrigued by the notion of making personal care products. And they're easy to make!

Deodorant

Deodorant is not the same as antiperspirant. (Antiperspirant has aluminum in it, which is what concerns some people.) Although deodorant won't keep you from sweating, it will help you smell fresher. (I've always figured that if God didn't want us to sweat, He would have made us without sweat glands. But He did…and sometimes we need a little help to stay pleasant smelling.) Instead of searching for straight deodorant (as opposed to deodorant/antiperspirant), why not make your own?

Alcohol or witch hazel. You may find it hard to believe, but using alcohol as a deodorant really works. Use either 99-percent isopropyl or 95-percent grain ethyl alcohol. *Note:* If you use this as a deodorant the same day you shave your underarms, I guarantee you'll wake up in a hurry. Witch hazel makes a good deodorant also, and it makes a passable aftershave too. I use alcohol quite often because it's so handy and does the job. Use a cotton ball to swab the alcohol or witch hazel on your skin. Let it dry before you put your top on. No mixing, no fuss, no muss—my kind of product!

Baking soda, cornstarch, and arrowroot powder. You can use baking soda alone or mix it with equal amounts of cornstarch and arrowroot powder. A little goes a long way, so use this mixture very sparingly. If the mixture causes irritation because you have sensitive skin, try using less baking soda or just use arrowroot and cornstarch. There's a lot of leeway on this recipe, so experiment until you find what works best for you.

Coconut oil, baking soda, cornstarch, and arrowroot. Use the kind of coconut oil that's solid at room temperature, although it tends to liquefy at 75 degrees or so. On hot days, consider keeping the coconut oil or coconut oil deodorant mixture you've made in the fridge. Here are two ways to use coconut oil. Again there is a lot of leeway in these recipes, so feel free to experiment with amounts until you find what works best for you.

- Rub a small amount of the coconut oil on your underarms. Use a powder puff to lightly dab on the baking soda or baking soda with equal amounts of cornstarch and arrowroot. Very easy to use but it can be a bit messy.

- Make a very thick paste with the coconut oil and baking soda/cornstarch or arrowroot mixture. I usually use about 2 tablespoons baking soda and two or three times that amount of cornstarch or arrowroot powder. First, mix together the powders you plan to use. Add the coconut oil, and mix with your hands. Work quickly because the coconut oil will melt once it comes into contact with your body heat. When you're making this, think about the moisture content. You don't want too much coconut oil, but you do want enough that when you use it, the mixture isn't crumbly. Use a pea-sized amount and rub it into your skin. (It takes very little to work!) Give it a few minutes to absorb before putting your clothes on. I find I get more even and thorough coverage when I rub it into my underarms. For storage, you can stuff this mixture into an empty deodorant tube (if using a recycled tube, make sure it's very clean) or put it in a small, covered container.

Hair Care

Store-bought shampoos are detergents that strip your hair of contaminants, but they also remove your natural hair oils. That's why you often need to use a conditioner after shampooing. Homemade shampoo, on the other hand, is a soap rather than a detergent, so you shouldn't need to use conditioner. However, you do need to rinse your hair with vinegar and water to get the soap residue completely out.

Liquid castile soap or Ivory soap, ¼ cup apple cider vinegar. The easiest way to get your hair clean is to use some liquid castile soap or rub a bar of Ivory soap over your wet hair and work up a lather. You will need to get every square inch of your scalp and hair soapy, because if you miss a place, that section won't get clean like it would if using a detergent. So take your time. It's a good idea to let the lather sit on your head for several minutes, so this might be a good time to soap the rest of your body with that bar of Ivory. Then rinse well. You will notice your hair feels as though the soap hasn't gotten completely out, and it will be tangled. (The liquid castile soap rinses out better.)

Now you're ready for the second step, which is to pour on a vinegar rinse. Use ¼ cup of apple cider vinegar in a quart of warm water. Pour it over your head and rinse as usual. This gets the soap residue out and makes your hair more manageable. I often cheat by keeping a squirt bottle of full-strength apple cider vinegar in the shower. I simply squirt it on my head and rinse. It works, but on cold winter mornings mixing the vinegar with warm water is a lot nicer than the shock of using the cold apple cider vinegar alone.

Remember the Economical Liquid Dish Soap recipe in the "Soap for the Kitchen" section of this chapter (see page 57)? Well, you can use it for shampoo, and it makes a great body wash. If you want to try a little fancier recipe for your personal care needs, try this.

◆ ◆ ◆ ◆

FANCY LIQUID SOAP FOR HAIR

¼ cup distilled or filtered soft water
¼ cup liquid castile soap (such as Dr. Bronner's)
½ tsp. light vegetable oil (optional)
⅛ tsp. essential oil (optional)

Mix together all ingredients and keep in an easy-to-use bottle or container. I recommend using a plastic squeeze bottle, such as the kind ketchup or mustard comes in. After washing your hair, rinse with apple cider vinegar and water. Your hair will come out wonderfully clean.

◆ ◆ ◆ ◆

Lip Balm

I love making lip balm. It's utterly satisfying, doesn't use much in the way of ingredients, and makes a wonderful gift. I keep some in my purse at all times, and in a pinch this homemade lip balm makes a great hand lotion.

½ cup almond or other vegetable oil (I sometimes use olive or coconut oil if I don't have almond oil handy)
½ oz. beeswax, finely grated (ends up being about 4 tablespoons)
1 to 2 tsp. honey (to taste)
1 tsp. vanilla extract (not absolutely necessary)

Place the vegetable oil and beeswax in a small saucepan and heat on low to medium-low until the beeswax melts. Remove from the burner and add the honey and vanilla. Stir well. Immediately pour into containers. The smaller the container the better. You want to be able to easily run your finger over the top to get the lip balm and apply it. If you want to get fancy, buy empty lip balm tubes or small pots with lids to pour the mixture into. (You'll need more than a dozen of these containers because they're very small.) The lip balm hardens as it cools. For faster cooling put filled containers in your refrigerator until the mixture sets.

Body Lotion

Want to try some body lotion that has no unpronounceable ingredients?

½ cup vegetable or olive oil
½ cup coconut oil (or ¼ cup cocoa butter and ¼ cup coconut oil)
½ cup beeswax, finely grated (measure grated, not packed down)
1 pint canning jar

Combine all ingredients in the canning jar. Add a little water to the saucepan, place the jar in the saucepan, and add more water until it comes at least halfway up the side of the canning jar. Be careful not to get water in the jar (water and oil don't mix). Turn the heat on medium-low and stir while the beeswax and coconut oil melt together. When the mixture is fully liquefied, remove the jar from the saucepan using hot pads and place in the refrigerator (on another hot pad) to cool and thicken. (Canning jars are made of tempered glass so they can go directly into the refrigerator.) Stir the lotion every 15 minutes for at least one hour (I use a timer).

Because the ingredients are so minimal, this lotion can be used on your face too. *Note:* A little goes a long way. After using this lotion, you might want to wait a few minutes before dressing to let the oils absorb into your skin.

4

Backyard Gardening

◆ ◆

*God said, "Behold, I have given you every plant yielding
seed that is on the surface of all the earth, and every tree
which has fruit yielding seed; it shall be food for you."*

GENESIS 1:29 NASB

Planting and tending a garden is as old as the Garden of Eden. God put Adam "into the garden of Eden to cultivate it and keep it" (Genesis 2:15 NASB). God gave humans the desire to nurture the soil and tend a spot of land. For many of us, that longing causes us to want a bit of dirt of our own to cultivate and care for so we can feed our families. "God saw all that He had made, and behold, it was very good" (Genesis 1:31 NASB). Gardeners agree!

◆ WHAT THE AMISH CAN TEACH US ◆

For the Amish, the question "What's for dinner?" is easily answered by looking toward the garden. Much of what an Amish family eats is produced on their own land. Fruits, vegetables, milk, eggs, grain, and livestock are tended and harvested. Food is plentiful, and appetites are hearty. Amish gardens are generally large and well tended. Row after neat row yields vegetables of all kinds, and flowers often brighten the edges of the plot. Fruiting plants, shrubs, and trees dot the landscape. For a would-be gardener, this vision seems like the perfect dream.

Unfortunately not everyone has access to large plots of land. Many of us live in towns or in suburbs with small yards, or in apartments or condos with only a patio or deck for outside space. But lack of a large available area doesn't have to stop us from growing at least some of our food at home. The only requirements for gardening are lots of sun, some soil outside or in containers (a large pot will do in a pinch), and a way to water the plants.

Years ago I lived in San Francisco while attending school. My apartment was on the third floor of an old building that had an old-fashioned fire escape I could access through my kitchen window. The fire escape got plenty of sunshine, so I hatched the idea of placing a few pots on the landing and growing a few vegetables—mostly lettuce and herbs. A few flowers rounded out my "garden spot."

I loved to start my day sitting at the kitchen table, holding my cup of coffee in my hands, and watching my tiny garden grow. I got as much satisfaction from that little plot of food and beauty in the city as I did in later years with my large garden in the country. Today I live in a small town, in a small house, that has a small yard. But I harvest much of what I eat during the growing season and have plenty to put by for the winter. True, I don't have the large swath of lawn that most of my neighbors do, but I can always wander outside when it comes time to answer the age-old question, "What's for dinner?"

Because there are entire books that teach how to garden successfully, I'm going to offer some suggestions that have worked for me. Like the Amish, I tend to garden with hand tools instead of using costly tools and gas-hungry gadgets some people believe are necessary to produce food. It takes more elbow grease my way, but time spent in the yard or on the patio happily fussing with your own plants is well worth the sore muscles. And as one of my friends likes to say, "Who needs a gym membership when you have a garden?"

Soil

Become a gardener, and you may find yourself waxing poetic about dirt. Good soil is foundational to good gardens, but most of us aren't lucky enough to live where the soil is rich, healthy, and full of the nutrients plants need to grow their best. We can help our gardens along by choosing to "grow" healthier soil over the years while we're growing fruits, flowers, and vegetables.

Compost

Imagine you're taking a walk in a forest or through open country untouched by humans. Notice that the ground isn't bare. There is a cushion of dead and decomposing organic matter. In fact, you can't see any dirt. If you dig through the cushion of organic matter, you'll notice that the layers of debris get smaller and more decomposed the further you dig. For the sake of our gardening adventure, we'll call this "natural compost," otherwise known as "black gold." This is what you want in your garden.

You can buy a truckload of compost from a local yard and garden center, but the cost can add up in a hurry. Purchasing that load of compost might be just the ticket if you're setting up a new garden spot and want to start planting right now. But for the long term, it's best to begin by making your own compost.

There are scientific ways to compost that allow you to go from garden debris to usable compost in a matter of weeks, but that takes more time and energy than many of us are willing to devote to the endeavor. So here is composting for the rest of us. I've used this method successfully for many years.

If desired, you can build a wooden structure with an open bottom and wooden slats on the sides that are placed far enough apart that air can get in between them but the debris won't fall out. This isn't necessary for creating a good compost pile. I have one bin my son built for me several years ago, and I love it, but I also have just piles of compost. Both ways work, but a bin helps contain the organic matter.

A compost pile needs to have at least three feet available in all directions—length, width, and height. Keep this in mind while you're building the pile. Don't go more than five feet in all directions or the pile will become too unwieldy to turn. You can place your compost pile in a shady part of the garden as long as it gets some sun during the day. I suggest placing your piles in less-than-optimal spots in your yard so you can maximize your garden growing area.

What goes into a compost pile. Toss in manure, leaves, grass clippings, garden debris (make sure the pieces are small or they'll take forever to decompose), coffee grounds, eggs shells, and kitchen food scraps.

What not to put into your compost pile. Don't put meat, bones, oil, cooking grease, and butter in your compost pile. Also don't include items that you're not sure where they've been so you don't inadvertently introduce heavy metals, pesticides, or other toxins into your soil.

Building your compost pile. When creating your compost pile, first layer the bottom with old cornstalks or larger pieces of garden waste to lift the pile off the ground a bit so air can circulate. Next, add these layers:

- 6 to 8 inches of organic materials (grass clippings, kitchen food scraps, garden debris, etc.)
- 2 inches of animal manure (from chickens, rabbits, horses, cows, etc., but never from meat-eating animals)
- 2 inches of brown material, such as straw, hay, or dried leaves
- a handful of garden soil every so often

And that's it. I turn the pile regularly during warmer months and pretty much leave it alone in the winter. If the weather is dry, add water to the pile so it doesn't dry out. The pile should be damp but not soggy. During the rainy season, cover the pile most of the time so it doesn't get waterlogged. Remember to take the cover off sometimes to keep the pile from getting too dry.

Once you begin turning your pile regularly, those nicely constructed layers are obliterated. With that in mind, I sometimes dump my waste into the pile as it comes. I won't get compost nearly as quickly, but everything does eventually decompose. Also, there have been seasons in my life when I didn't have access to free manure so I didn't add it. Coffee grounds are a proven and good substitute. If you don't drink coffee, many espresso stands will save their grounds for you if you ask, provide the bucket, and pick the grounds up regularly. And when you harvest your lovely homegrown produce, take the baristas some. They'll appreciate it.

Green Manure

Green manuring is basically growing a crop and then plowing it back under so the plant matter will enrich the soil as it decomposes. If you use a tiller for your garden, planting a green manure cover crop to overwinter and help build the soil is a great practice. You can plant a cover crop for green manure in raised beds, but in the spring turning all that plant material into the soil by hand is hard work.

Generally cover crops are planted in the fall after the ground is harvested or very early in the spring, depending on where you live. In my location, crimson clover is probably the number one choice for home gardeners, but gardeners also use alfalfa, peas, vetch, millet, buckwheat, and similar plants. The key is to use plants with fast-growing seeds that grow in the cool weather.

When it's time to till in the cover crop, you may need to scythe or mow first if the growth is luxuriant and tall. When you've finished tilling the cover crop into the soil, let the area sit until the plant residues have time to decompose. A month is good, but your area may differ, so ask experienced local gardeners what works best in your climate zone.

Manure

If you live near an Amish settlement, you've no doubt seen Amish farmers spreading manure over their fields. They are fertilizing. There's no need for them to go to the local farm store to buy bags of chemicals to enhance their soil. Their fertilizer "store" is right in the barn. If you have access to manure, use it. In fact, if you want to or are growing your own food and want gorgeous flowers and shrubs in the bargain, keep some chickens or rabbits in the backyard (see chapter 5, "Raising Backyard Livestock").

"Hot" manure, the stuff that comes directly from the animals, is generally too rich for plants. (The exception to this rule is rabbit manure, which is considered "cold," and therefore safe to apply directly to your garden.) Hot manure will burn plants due to the ammonia present, so the manure needs to be aged first. You can build a manure pile and let it sit for months or you can put it in your compost pile and get it in usable shape in less time. No matter which way you go, you must let manure compost before applying it to your garden. If you build a manure pile, make sure it doesn't get rained on, which would leach out the nutrients. Conversely, you also need to keep it from getting completely dried out. Cover the manure during wet seasons with soil or a tarp, and in dry weather give it a spritz with the hose now and again.

I've had success "side-dressing" my plants and trees with composted manure. (Side-dressing is simply placing plant nutrients on or in the soil near the roots of a plant.) If I have enough fertilizer left, I broadcast or spread it over my entire garden area and till it in.

Homemade Fertilizer

If you don't have animals and don't want to bother getting manure, you can always go to a local garden center and pick up bags of fertilizer or finished compost. However, the cost can add up quickly. A less expensive way to get the good stuff into your soil is by making your own fertilizer. The following recipe for one gallon of fertilizer works well. (I buy the ingredients in 50-pound sacks at a local feed and farm store. I save a lot of money by buying in bulk, and I store the unused portion in a safe, dry place.)

1 quart seed meal (you can use cottonseed or soybean meal)
1 quart greensand
½ quart dolomite or ½ quart dry agricultural lime, or a combination
    of both

1 quart bone meal (optional)
½ quart gypsum (optional)

Using a quart container, measure out the ingredients and place in a large container with a sealable lid. Mix everything together well. Label the container "Homemade Fertilizer" and list the ingredients. Store in a safe, dry place.

I use about a gallon of the mixed fertilizer per 100 square feet at the beginning of the growing season and work it into the first few inches of soil with a hoe. Occasionally I'll side-dress a small amount into the soil around heavy feeders (such as tomatoes) during the growing season.

Planning Your Garden

Often the size of our gardens is limited by the amount of space we have available. But if you're starting a new garden, and especially if you've never gardened before, think "smaller is better." It's much easier to gain gardening skills with a manageable space rather than attempting a large garden in your first year and becoming overwhelmed by all the weeding, watering, and harvesting. Those big, beautiful gardens that dot the Amish landscape are the result of many years of experience. Youngsters have grown up helping with the family garden, and by the time they are adults they know what to do and how much to plant to feed their own growing households.

Container Gardening

Container gardening is a great boon to those with limited space or for people with physical limitations who would have difficulty working in a regular garden. This type of gardening works well if you have a small patio or deck. Or maybe you have a lot of space available but having a few greens growing in a pot is all you need to satisfy your green thumb.

Pots, barrels, and planter boxes. You can plant almost any vegetable in a container as long as it is deep enough to allow the roots to grow, a minimum of 6 to 8 inches, but deeper is better. It's especially useful for fast-growing or cut-and-come-again veggies, such as radishes, beet greens, chard, lettuce, spinach, and some herbs. Almost any container will work as a pot. You'll need to water your plants more often than if you had a regular garden, especially in hot weather. I buy pots with holes in them to provide plenty of drainage so water won't collect and cause the roots to rot. If your pot or barrel is large enough, you can even grow tomatoes or trellis pole beans, peas, and cucumbers.

Bags of soil. I read an article several years back that advocated growing veggies in store-bought bags of soil that are laid on top of where you want a new garden site to be. Over the growing season, you get to harvest some food, and the plastic bags will suffocate the weeds and grass underneath, making the soil easier to prepare for a permanent bed. I tried it with some success. Bags are also a good option on a patio or deck if you don't have access to pots or barrels. Grow only short-rooted plants though. Tomatoes won't work in such limited depth.

Poke several holes in what will be the "bottom" of the bag for drainage. Lay the bags snug up next to each other or, if using only one bag, set boards along the two long edges to keep the soil from sprawling and flattening when you cut a slit along the top of the bag to plant.

Bunch each bag up so the sides won't fall wide open when you make the top cuts.

Now make a long cut down the center of the bag, along with two smaller, perpendicular cuts near each short end (it will look like a wide "H" when you're done). Peel back the plastic to allow more soil to show.

Wet the soil, and let the water fully absorb before planting.

Plant, water, and watch your plants grow.

Raised Beds

Raised beds are great for small spaces, for areas where the ground is less than ideal, and for people who have mobility concerns because they won't have to bend down so far to work. The downside of raised beds, in my opinion, is the cost of the lumber and nails, building them or finding a willing handyperson to get the job done, and getting the soil needed to fill them.

You can use wood or composite (plastic) for the frame. Never use old railroad ties or treated lumber because the chemicals used are toxic and can leach into your garden. I've seen quite a few people over the years use old railroad ties, but I won't risk my family's health…even if I can get the ties for free. I'm sure you feel the same way.

If you'd like to make an old-fashioned wooden garden bed, follow these instructions.

First, decide what size of garden you want. Any size will work, but I've found that garden beds that are approximately 8 feet by 4 feet work well.

Buy six 2 x 6 x 8 boards. Cedar, redwood, or cypress are good to use because they have some natural rot resistance.

Saw two of the boards in half.

You now have four 8-foot boards and four 4-foot boards. You're going to start by making two rectangular boxes of the same size.

With the wide sides vertical, place a 4-foot board at the end of an 8-foot board at right angles to form a corner. Use screws or nails to connect the boards to each other. I think screws work better than nails. If you use screws, you'll find it helpful to get them started in the first board before placing it next to the second board and screwing them together. (You might need another set of hands for this step to get the angles sharp.) Repeat until you have 2 equal-sized boxes. You're making two 6-inch-high, rectangular wooden box frames.

When you're done, move them to their permanent spot. Place one box exactly where you want the raised bed to be. Then set the second rectangular box directly on top of the first one so you now have one box with sides a foot high.

Get some sturdy stakes (2 x 2 boards work well and hold up to the elements). Heavy metal stakes or lengths of rebar are even better. Pound a stake on the inside of each corner of the box. Then put two stakes on the outside of each corner. The idea is to keep the boards steady so they can't wobble inward or outward or fall over. It's like a board sandwich at each corner. You can also put stakes in the middle of the 8-foot lengths for added sturdiness.

Fill your new garden bed with good compost and soil. Get planting!

Another kind of raised bed I've used for many years doesn't cost anything to implement and it's easy to do. When you prepare your garden in the spring, simply "hill up the dirt" into raised beds and plant as usual. You can make them any length or width that suits you. Because the soil isn't stepped on and compacted during the season, you can plant more intensively. Drainage is also better in raised beds, so this is a good choice for areas that get a fair amount of rainfall during the gardening season. The downside to these raised beds is that you'll have to weed by hand or hoe very carefully so you don't degrade the sides of the hills. If it gets very hot in your area, you may need to water more often.

Hills

A "hill" is clustering a group of like plants together. Sometimes gardeners actually create tiny hills 6 to 8 inches higher than the surrounding ground and then plant the cluster of plants. In hot, windy areas, a hill can also be a depression of 6 to 8 inches to better hold and direct the available water to the plants and protect the seedlings from drying and shredding winds.

The usual crops planted in hills are the vining and climbing types, such as melons, squash, cucumbers, and pole beans. With the exception of pole beans, these plants are space hogs, so plan accordingly. Picture each hill as the center of an imaginary circle. The vines will grow outward in all directions and eventually take up the available space. When I use hills for melons, squash, and cucumbers, after the plants have a good start I generally thin them down to three plants per hill.

Traditional Rows

In traditional row gardening you plant long rows of vegetables in a single line down the center of the row. The garden looks neat, and weeding is easy between the plants and between those long rows. You don't need to buy or build anything special to have a row garden! If you start reading gardening books and magazines, you'll soon learn that row gardening wastes a lot of space. At least half of the garden area is taken up by the paths between each row. The typical row garden also doesn't use water efficiently unless you flood irrigate between the rows, which most home gardeners don't do.

Still, if you have the space, a traditional row garden is a thing of beauty. You might want to give it a try.

Seed Planting—Outside and Inside

These seeds can be planted directly in your garden: beans, beets, carrots, chard, corn, kohlrabi, lettuce and other greens, peas, potatoes, pumpkins, radishes, squash, and turnips.

Not all vegetable seeds can be successfully planted directly into the garden. Some need to be started indoors and then transplanted outside. These include broccoli, Brussels sprouts, cabbage, cauliflower, celery, cucumbers, eggplant, herbs, leeks, melons, onions, peppers, and tomatoes.

This list isn't exhaustive, nor is it set in stone. In your particular area, you might be able to directly sow some of these seeds. You can get advice for planting from a garden expert at a store that handles garden supplies, check out a book from the library on gardening in your area, or ask a master gardener through your local extension service.

Seed Starting

There's nothing wrong with heading to the garden center or nursery for your plant starts in the spring. In fact, that's an excellent way to begin because someone else has taken the trouble to get those little seedlings ready for transplanting into your garden. You don't need to amass the equipment and get the know-how needed to start seeds or figure out when they must be planted to be the right size when it's time to be planted outside. The drawback is that you will have far fewer choices available regarding what varieties to plant because most garden centers concentrate on a few varieties proven for their area. At some point you may want to grow seeds from scratch. And once you have the necessary equipment, planting from seeds can save you tons of money.

Seed starting mix. You can use garden soil or regular potting mix to start seeds, but you'll have much better results if you purchase a specially formulated seed starting mix or make your own. To make your own seed starting mix use equal parts of vermiculite, peat moss or coconut coir, and perlite. You can get away with not using the perlite if you want to save money, but it's better to include it.

Water down the soil or starting mix until it's spongy but not soggy. Let it sit for a bit so the particles have time to absorb the water.

You'll need to have a container to allow for drainage. You can buy seedling trays or reuse something you have that will fill the bill. Trays with little dividers to keep the roots separate to make transplanting easier is best. Fill the trays with your soil or potting mixture.

Plant the seeds. Plant two seeds in each cell of your seed planting tray. This allows for better germination rates per unit. Plant the seeds on top of the bed and lightly sprinkle with more seed starting mix. If both seeds come up (a likely occurrence) and once two or three sets of leaves have formed, pick the one that looks the healthiest and snip out the weaker one with a sharp pair of scissors. (You don't want to pull it out by the roots because that might damage the seedling left behind.)

Cover the tray. Cover the tray with plastic or the plastic dome that came with it. Place the tray somewhere warm. On top of the refrigerator is a good spot or in a warm room in your house. Don't worry just yet about providing light because until the seedlings emerge they don't need any.

If a lot of moisture has formed on the inside of the cover, prop the lid open for an hour or two each day. But also make sure the soil doesn't dry out. Bottom water or gently mist if you need to add water.

Providing light. When the seedlings start emerging, remove the plastic cover and place the tray where the plants will get light. You can buy a grow light system with a special fluorescent tube, but those can be expensive. An alternative is to buy a fluorescent shop light fixture, the kind that are four feet long or so and hold two tubes. Buy the "cool white" tubes. Keep the light on the plants for approximately 16 hours per day. Position the light one or two inches above the seedlings, and keep moving the light up (or the trays down) as the seedlings grow.

Feed the seedlings. Every two weeks, feed the seedlings a diluted liquid fertilizer, such as fish emulsion or compost tea.

Repot in larger containers. If the plants seem to be getting too big for the cells, repot them into larger pots or trays. A 4-inch pot will usually do until time to plant the seedlings outdoors.

Harden off. When it gets close to the time when you'll be planting the seedlings outdoors, move the trays or pots outside for several hours during the warmest part of the day. Each day or two, lengthen the time they stay outside so they can adjust to the bright sunlight. Do this for at least a week.

Tips for Creating a Great Garden

- Know your "plant hardiness zone." This will help you to choose plant varieties that are suited to your climate. You can find an updated hardiness zone map at http://plant hardiness.ars.usda.gov or ask a garden person at a local nursery or garden store.

- Plants need an inch of water per week during the growing season. This can come from rain or from irrigation. How do you know what one inch of water is? Take a straight-sided cake pan and set it in your garden. Measure the water level as you irrigate or after it rains, and you'll get a fairly close estimate.

- Plant taller vegetables away from the sun so they don't shade out lower growing plants. In the northern hemisphere, this is the north side of your garden. In the southern hemisphere, plant the taller plants on the south side of your garden.

- Situate the majority of your garden in a sunny place. If you include slightly shaded areas, you can grow leafy greens such as lettuce, chard, and spinach.

- You don't need to plant everything at once. If you plant in succession, you won't be overwhelmed with everything ripening at once. For instance, by planting three batches of green beans two weeks apart, you'll extend the harvest, have more managable quantities at any given time, and stretch out your eating enjoyment.

- Grow the vegetables you know your family will eat. You can experiment with one or two new vegetables, but in general stick to what you know will get eaten.

- Don't neglect fertilizing your garden during the growing season. Side-dress plants with a natural fertilizer or compost midway through their growth.

- Don't plant the same veggies in the same spots year after year. Instead, rotate their placement in the garden. Disease organisms can overwinter in the soil and gain the upper hand in no time against young seedlings.

- Mulch your garden. Cover the soil around your plants to a depth of two inches. You can use seed-free straw or other organic material. A layer of mulch suppresses weeds and keeps the soil underneath moist so you won't have to water as often.

- Stay on top of the weeding. Not only is it a psychological boost when you survey your weed-free garden, but your plants will grow more vigorously when they don't compete for food and water.

- Plant some flowers with your veggies. They will add color and beauty to the garden as well as attract beneficial insects. Try using edible flowers—they'll do double duty. These include marigolds, nasturtiums, sunflowers, pansies, bee balm, lavender, Johnny-jump-ups, carnations, English daisies, and borage. For a garnish, you can use the entire flower, but if you plan to eat them, they usually taste better if you only use the petals.

- Keep a journal. It can be a valuable tool for future gardens. It's also great fun to reread your entries from past years to remind yourself of what worked and what didn't. Don't forget to record weather patterns (they can vary considerably from year to year) and anything you might want to remember down the road.

Extended Season Gardening

There are tricks and tools you can use to extend the gardening season so you can have something fresh to eat for most of the year. The first way is to construct a greenhouse. If that's not an option because of time, space, and money, there are some alternatives.

Cloches and Hoop Tunnels

Cloches were originally glass bell jars that were placed over single plants, creating a mini greenhouse. They do work, and today cloches come in glass and plastic and can be shaped like bells, domes, and tunnels. Cloches can be quite expensive, but you can also make your own using two-liter pop bottles or gallon milk jugs. Just cut the bottom off and stick the top part over the plant and into the ground. You can leave the cap on, but you'll need to watch carefully that it doesn't get too hot inside. If it does, you can take the cap off on warm or sunny days. Cloches are best used in early spring for tender, young plants that need some protection from cold temperatures.

Hoop tunnels are higher, so they can accommodate taller plants. They don't offer much in the way of protection from very cold weather, but if you live in an area that doesn't get too cold they can be a great asset. To make a homemade hoop tunnel, get some eight-foot-long pieces of ¾- to 1-inch PVC pipe. You'll need one for every 2 to 3 feet of planting surface.

Starting at the end of a row, every 2 to 3 feet pound some rebar or other sturdy stakes into the ground in pairs, one on each side of the row. Make them about four feet apart, and at a slight inward angle. Slip the end of the PVC pipe over one stake, and then the other end of the PVC pipe on the other side, bending the plastic pipe into a hoop shape. Cover the hoops with plastic sheeting, the thicker the better to offer more protection from the cold. Make sure you can open the ends for ventilation. Once you've spread out the plastic, clip it to the pipe at intervals to hold it in place. There are clips made for this purpose, and they are a good investment. You'll need to secure the bottom in some way. I've stapled the plastic to lengths of lumber, and I've also held it in place with large rocks.

Cold Frames and Hot Beds

Cold frames are small glass- or plastic-covered growing beds that rely on the sun for their heat source. There are many cold frame designs available, or you can buy them as kits or preassembled. But an easy and inexpensive idea for making a cold frame uses straw and a piece of glass, such as an old window (preferably still in its frame).

Make a square with four bales of straw, or you can use 6 bales total and make a rectangle if your glass is large enough to span the top. That's really all you have to do, but I've found that if I dig down on the south side (toward the sun) so the bales sit on the ground at an angle, the sun can shine into the front part of the cold frame much better. My straw bale cold frames last the winter, and then I use the straw as mulch or as building material for my compost pile.

If you choose to make a cold frame out of wood (you can also use opaque plastic for the sides), the higher north end should be about 18 inches tall, and the southern end should be around 12 inches in height. Place a glass or plastic lid over the frame, making sure the hinge is on the north side. You'll need some way to prop open the lid on sunny days when the temperature rises above 45 degrees. Lower the lid early enough in the afternoon to build up some heat for keeping the plants warm when the temperature drops at night. When the temperature is predicted to drop to below freezing, it's a good idea to cover the glass top with old blankets or burlap bags filled with leaves. You can insulate the sides of a wooden or plastic cold frame with soil or straw, but if you make your cold frame out of straw bales you've got built-in insulation.

Slugs can be a problem in a cold frame, so patrol regularly and dispose of them immediately. You can set a margarine tub filled with flat beer into the ground inside the frame. They'll crawl into it and drown. Or use a mixture of ¼ cup honey and 1 teaspoon yeast mixed into a cup of boiling water (heat and stir until the honey has melted and thoroughly mixed in with the water), and place this inside the frame.

It may be raining buckets outside, but you'll need to monitor the moisture level of the soil *inside* the cold frame and add water occasionally. You might want to give the plants a watering with diluted fertilizer too.

Cold frames are used during the winter months to grow cool-weather crops such as petite carrots, radishes, lettuce, spinach, kale, and other leafy greens. Wouldn't it be nice to enjoy a fresh salad from your garden with Christmas dinner? It's possible!

Hot beds are simply cold frames that have a bottom heat source, either heating cables or fresh manure dug into the root zone area and then topped with soil. The manure heats as it composts and keeps the roots of the plants inside the cold frame warm. Use about a foot-deep layer of fresh manure topped with at least 6 inches of soil if you want to turn your cold frame into a hot bed.

Seed Saving

For many gardeners, buying an annual supply of vegetable and flower seeds from a catalog or garden center is a time-honored and enjoyable winter ritual. But why not save some seeds from this year's harvest for planting next year? Saving seeds isn't difficult if you know what to do, and you will save money because you have your ready-made seed supply store right in the garden. Saving seeds isn't for everyone, but learning how to do so can give you a self-reliance boost and ensure that those tasty beans your grandmother planted when you were a child will be available to your own grandchildren.

One of the best books on the subject is *Seed to Seed: Seed Saving and Growing Techniques for Vegetable Gardens* by Suzanne Ashworth. Get the updated edition, which lists 160 different vegetables.

Open Pollinated vs. Hybrid Seeds

Open pollinated seeds haven't been modified or altered in any unnatural way. You can be confident that seeds planted next year will reproduce true to type, meaning next year's veggies will look and taste just the same as this year's. Saving your own seeds year after year will produce plants that are optimally adapted to your microclimate because they came from your particular set of growing conditions. And you can help matters along because you decide what seeds to save—maybe some seeds from the plant that gave you extra large tomatoes or the beans you were able to harvest in spite of a short growing season.

Hybrid seeds come from plants that have been deliberately crosspollinated. If you were to save the seeds of a hybrid plant, you might not get what you were expecting because the next generation of a hybrid plant doesn't reproduce true to type. If you don't care about saving seeds, planting hybrids can be wonderful. They generally grow vegetables that are more like grocery store produce, so your family won't be put off when you serve vegetables for dinner. And "hybrid vigor" means you'll likely have plants that are more productive than the open pollinated varieties.

If you want to save your own seeds, you'll definitely want to plant open pollinated seeds. When you're reading seed packets or going through your seed catalogs, choose varieties that say "OP" or "open pollinated." Hybrid varieties will say "hybrid" or possibly "F1." Sometimes you'll see seeds marked "heirloom." These are good choices for seed saving also. And by growing the older, open pollinated varieties, you will be protecting plant genetic diversity.

Seed Catalogs

Most gardeners love looking through seed catalogs. Reading them is especially enjoyable in the dead of winter when the snow flies and it's cold outside. And as you study what's available, you'll also get an education in so much more because these catalogs are chock-full of valuable information. Here are some seed catalogs you might want to look over.

- *Botanical Interests, Inc.;* www.botanicalinterests.com; 660 Compton Street, Broomfield, CO, 80020; 877-821-4340.

- *Bountiful Gardens;* www.bountifulgardens.org; 1726-D South Main Street, Willits, CA 95490; 707-459-6410.

- *Burpee Seeds and Plants;* www.burpee.com; 300 Park Avenue, Warminster, PA 18974; 1-800-888-1447.

- *Fedco Seeds;* www.fedcoseeds.com; PO Box 520, Waterville, ME 04903; 207-873-7333 or 207-430-1106.

- *Ferry-Morse Seed Co.;* www.ferry-morse.com; 601 Stephen Beale Drive, Fulton, KY 42041; 800-626-3392.

- *Gurney's Seed & Nursery Co.;* www.gurneys.com; PO Box 4178, Greendale, IN 47025-4178; 513-354-1492.

- *Johnny's Selected Seeds;* www.johnnyseeds.com; 955 Benton Avenue, Winslow, ME 04901; 877-564-6697.

- *Nichols Garden Nursery;* www.nicholsgardennursery.com; 1190 Old Salem Road NE, Albany, OR 97321; 800-422-3985.

- *Seed Saver's Exchange;* www.seedsavers.org; 3094 North Winn Road, Decorah, IA 52101; 563-382-5990.

- *Seeds of Change;* www.seedsofchange.com; PO Box 4908, Rancho Dominguez, CA 90220; 888-762-7333.

- *Territorial Seed Co.;* www.territorialseed.com; PO Box 158, Cottage Grove, OR 97424; 800-626-0866.

There are many, many more seed companies out there, but this list is a good start. Right around the beginning of the year is a good time to check for new catalogs to be available. Begin the new year right by sending away for seed catalogs to start planning your summer garden!

Coping with Pests and Disease

Many of us like to grow our food in part because we're concerned about food safety. Using pesticides, chemical fertilizers, and insecticides to deal with pest and disease damage negates many of the reasons why we garden organically. This becomes even more important if our available space is small because children and pets are more likely to be exposed to any toxic chemicals used in the garden area.

Forgoing the use of chemicals has many benefits. You'll save money by not purchasing these products, and you can feel good about not adding to the load of synthetic chemicals that find their way into our soils and waterways, harming wildlife and beneficial insect populations in the process. Plus, you'll have no worries when you wander out to the garden, pluck a sun-warmed tomato from a plant, and take a tasty, juicy bite.

There are effective, organic ways to deal with pests and disease. First and foremost is building and maintaining healthy soil. Healthy soil grows healthy plants. And healthy plants are more likely to resist diseases and pests. And don't forget that when you have healthy soil, you're able to garden more intensively—a boon to small spaces. And that equals more food for your family.

A good philosophy in the garden is to learn to live with some imperfections. Remember, for instance, that bad bugs quite often get eaten by beneficial bugs. In spite of our best efforts, there will be times when the bugs or diseases seem to be winning. That is the time to intervene. Here are some positive action steps you can take.

- *Know the bugs.* Just because you find a bug in the garden, that doesn't mean it's a garden enemy. For example, lady bug larvae look like fierce black-and-orange predators, but you want them in your garden.

- *Build healthy soil.* This is your first line of defense.

- *Use beneficial insects.* Ladybugs and nematodes can be purchased in some garden stores or online.

- *Rotate crops.* If you plant the same veggies in the same spots year after year, you will deplete the soil of certain key nutrients and give pests and diseases a head start on overwhelming fragile seedlings.

- *Hand pick bugs.* Gently remove bugs by hand and dispose of them.

- *Use physical barriers.* Put up physical barriers to keep bugs away from plants. These can be cardboard or aluminum foil collars placed around a plant and buried an inch or two into the soil. Floating row covers will keep out flying insects and birds, but they also won't allow effective pollination. Cloches, fences, and the like will also help.

- *Use baits and traps.* Slugs and snails seem to live in most gardens and can wipe out tender plants in a night. So can earwigs. Use baits to lure pests to their demise or trap them for removal later. These baits can be nontoxic, such as using beer in a shallow dish, which attracts snails and slugs, or laying boards out and then squishing what's underneath in the morning.

- *Plant trap crops.* These are crops that you plant to lure targeted bugs away from your real crop. Ask your local county extension worker about trap crops that might work in your area. Timing is important with trap crops. They need to be in place when the pest population is present.

- *Make use of companion planting.* Having diverse plantings that include flowers (nasturtiums and French marigolds are good choices) will help confuse and disperse insects.

- *No overhead watering.* If possible, water plants from below. Also, water at the best time of day for your area. In hot and windy locales, watering in the evening will help the water soak into the soil instead of evaporating. In soggy areas, it's better to water in the early morning so plants aren't wet all night long and prone to rot.

- *Use diatomaceous earth.* Diatomaceous earth is an all-natural product made from tiny fossilized water plants. Finely ground, it's a mineral-based pesticide. (Although it's a natural product, avoid breathing the dust.) This product will wreak havoc on soft-bodied pests (like those slugs). Sprinkle around plants or around the perimeter of your garden.

If you decide you want to use a bug spray, here's a good all-purpose, nontoxic-to-humans-and-pets spray:

1 quart hot water
10 garlic cloves
1 onion
1 tsp. cayenne pepper powder or 2 jalapenos
½ tsp. liquid soap (castile, dish soap, or laundry soap)

Blend all ingredients except the soap in the hot water. Mix well. Let sit covered on your counter overnight.

Strain the mixture through cheesecloth. Add the liquid soap and stir to mix, and then pour the liquid into a spray container. Label the container "BUG SPRAY! Do not drink!" Next add a list of ingredients so you have the recipe handy when you need to make more.

Spray a small amount on one leaf to make sure the pepper doesn't burn the tender plant. If it doesn't, drench the leaves and stems of the insect-infested plants.

Store the bug spray in your refrigerator, tightly covered, for up to a month.

If you've tried everything but your problem still exists, then it may be time to head down to the garden center for a commercial product. There are safe or minimally toxic choices available in stores today if you carefully follow the directions. Ask their garden experts for recommendations.

Seasoned gardeners soon learn to plant "one for the cutworm, one for the crow, one to rot, and one to grow."

5

Raising Backyard Livestock

◆ ◆

Be sure you know the condition of your flocks,
give careful attention to your herds.

PROVERBS 27:23

When the conversation turns to backyard livestock, your first thought might be about cows. For many of us, raising a cow or two just isn't feasible. One cow needs at least an acre of good pasture, and the fences better be well built and high enough to keep a jumper at home. Paying a butchering service can be expensive, and butchering a cow yourself is hard labor. The resulting 500 to 600 pounds of meat must be stored somewhere, and the leftovers must be disposed of.

If you choose to keep a milk cow, someone needs to be home in the morning and evening every single day to milk her. And the approximately 20 metric tons of manure one cow produces over the course of the year might be enough to fertilize every garden in your entire neighborhood.

Most of us don't live on acreage. Instead, more than 80 percent of us live in cities or suburbs and have little or no land on which to raise animals. Depending on your town's ordinances, there are some small food animals you can raise even if your yard is small. Chickens, rabbits, and bees are good examples. Increasingly, cities and suburbs across

America are changing their regulations so residents can keep at least a few chickens. This is good for all of us—one more link in the chain toward self-sufficiency.

There are plenty of options for suburban and city dwellers when it comes to raising backyard animals. One beehive can produce as much as 50 pounds of honey in a year, and the bees pollinate flowers, trees, and vegetables for several miles around their hives. The average hen lays around 220 eggs a year. A rabbit can easily produce 35 babies in that same time. The manure from chickens and rabbits provides great garden fertilizer in the bargain. And if you still yearn for backyard milk, you can always raise a pygmy milk goat and get approximately three quarts of rich, sweet-tasting milk every day.

◆ What the Amish Can Teach Us ◆

Morning comes early for the Amish. There are horses to feed, cows to milk, and eggs to gather before breakfast. Even those who don't farm for a living keep a driving horse or two; possibly a cow for milk, cream, butter, and cheese; and chickens, turkeys, ducks, and geese for meat, eggs, and feathers. A pig or two means ham, bacon, and plenty of lard for baking and soap making.

The Amish feel closer to God in the country and their rural lifestyle. They have learned to live with less and provide much of what they need for daily consumption right on their farms. Raising their own meat is one of the ways the Amish practice self-reliance and sustainability.

Like the Amish, you too can raise livestock. Raising some chickens or keeping bees isn't any more difficult than maintaining a garden. Bear in mind, that if you decide to go into animal husbandry, you are responsible for the animals you raise. They count on you to feed and water them and keep their homes clean and dry. And if you have neighbors who live nearby, they will appreciate you keeping your animals well maintained so they aren't bothered by noise, odor, or flies. A noisy rooster that crows at first light or goats that escape into the neighbors' yards and decimate their flowerbeds won't sit well with the people who live next to you. Thankfully, a dozen fresh eggs or a casserole made from your homegrown meat usually goes a long way toward gaining the interest and support of others. You might just start a trend.

Chickens

Raising a few chickens for their eggs is easy and downright delightful. I've had dozens of chickens over the years and loved many of them, but my favorite was Gwendolyn. (We christened her "Gw-HEN-dolyn," but called her Gwen for short.) She was a Plymouth Barred Rock hen—a black-and-white speckled beauty. She laid eggs well, which was a bonus, although by the time she was mature enough for us to know that, she had clucked her way into our hearts. We wouldn't have been able to "put her in the stew pot" if she turned out to be a poor egg layer.

Gwen was incredibly friendly, and when one of us ventured outside, she'd come running, hoping for pets and a treat. She'd fuss and squawk until we sat down and held her in our lap, and then she'd settle down and cluck contentedly while we gave her a good rub. Gwen was perfectly content to sleep in the henhouse at night, but I'm not really sure she ever believed she was a chicken. She was great friends with our dogs and cat, and they'd all pal around together scaring up bugs and field mice (a treat for all of them!) during the day. When my kids came into the house from playing, they were often accompanied by the dogs and cat…and Gwen, who'd troop indoors with the gang as if she belonged inside. I was forever shooing her out.

Gwen was with us for almost eight years, and for several of those years she was too old to reliably lay eggs. But we happily fed her and cared for her and considered her one of the family. She is a perfect example of how rewarding owning backyard livestock can be.

Chickens Come in All Sizes

There are different sizes of chickens, and they can be used for different purposes.

Broilers are your basic meat bird. They are bred to put on meat quickly so you can butcher them when they reach 8 to 10 weeks old. They are topnotch at converting feed to weight. If you want to raise birds for meat production, broilers will be your best investment. Broilers are generally white with yellow skin, which, when plucked, will yield a clean looking carcass. Cornish Rocks and Cornish crosses are the usual varieties. The Cornish game hens that you see for sale in grocery stores are simply Cornish Rock broilers that were butchered at 4 weeks of age.

Heavy chickens are good egg layer/meat combination birds. Most of the heavy breeds lay brown eggs that are good sized. Heavy breeds can withstand colder temperatures. They are generally more docile than the lighter breeds, and make good choices for families with children. Some of the more common breeds in the heavy category include Plymouth, White, and Barred Rocks; Rhode Island, New Hampshire, and Production Reds; Wyandottes; Orpingtons; Australorps; Ameraucanas; and Sussex. Many of the heritage breeds we associate with farmyards are in the heavy category.

Light and Bantam breeds are smaller birds that can be good layers although their eggs are small (it takes three bantam eggs to equal two regular eggs). They aren't good meat birds because of their small body size, and they tend to be more nervous and standoffish than the heavy breeds. Light birds include any of the bantam breeds, Leghorns, Araucanas, Minorcas, and Sicilian Buttercups. The eggs of light breeds are generally white. Light breeds often have beautiful plumage patterns, which can be a plus in a small backyard flock because they are fun to watch.

For a small backyard flock, the heavy breeds are the best option. Within the heavy category, heritage breeds are probably your best choice because they haven't had their natural tendencies bred out of them like many modern production breeds. They produce a good number of large eggs, and, in my experience, they have the best personalities. They don't fluster as easily and are somewhat quieter than the lighter breeds, which makes for better relations with any close neighbors and easier handling for you.

Getting Started

What came first—the chicken or the egg? That's a question you'll have to answer if you decide to get into keeping chickens. Chicks can be mail-ordered from a hatchery and arrive as "day old" chicks at your local post office, or you can buy them at your local feed and farm store. If you have a mama hen and a rooster to fertilize the eggs, you can let the hen brood and hatch out new chicks for you. Or you can find someone who is selling off their flock of layers and get adults instead of raising them yourself. There are pluses to each of these options.

Hatchery chicks. The choices available through hatcheries are wide-ranging, and if you have a specific breed of chicken in mind, this could be your best bet. Keep in mind that hatcheries generally have a minimum order requirement of 25 chicks because any fewer and they'll get too cold in transit. (Baby chicks *must* stay warm.) If you plan on having a large flock of one kind of bird, this is a good way to go.

Feed and farm store chicks. This is a great option for the small landholder. You can order any number of chicks from the store, and they'll let you know when they are due to arrive. The downside is that stores generally order only a few different breeds, so your selections may be somewhat limited. The upside is that these chicks will often be well suited to your locale. (In recent years, feed stores have been ordering a greater variety of breeds because backyard chickens have become very popular, so this is less of a problem than it was even ten years ago.) No order is too small at the feed store because they buy in bulk, but you should always plan on buying at least three chicks. Chickens flock together, and they do not thrive when they're alone. Sadly, baby chicks can die fairly easily in the first few weeks, so it's a good idea to have one or two more than you really need.

Keeping a rooster. Allowing a "broody" hen to set a nest and hatch out chicks is the most natural way to go, but most towns ban roosters from backyard flocks due to their crowing.

Incubate fertile eggs. Not all hens are broody, so it can be frustrating to get a nest set and chicks to hatch, especially if you can't keep a rooster on the premises. However, you can buy or barter for fertilized eggs and mechanically incubate them. Or you can incubate your own flock's fertilized eggs if your hens aren't broody. Watching baby chicks hatch can be enjoyable and educational, but incubators are a large investment. If you're on a tight budget, this option probably isn't for you. And if you only want three or four layers every few years, it's far more cost effective to buy day-old chicks instead.

Straight run, pullets, or cockerels? When you buy your chicks, you can buy straight run, pullets, or cockerels. Straight run means you get what's sent, whether that ends up being pullets (females) or cockerels (males) or, more than likely, a combination of both. In theory, a straight run order will give you 50 percent of each sex, but it doesn't always work out that way. If your aim is to raise chickens for egg laying, it's a good idea to spend the extra money and make sure you get all pullets. But even then you might be surprised a few months down the road when one of your "hens" starts crowing. It happens. Buy cockerels if your aim is to put meat in the freezer.

Brooding Chicks

Let's say you've decided to get some day-old chicks at your local feed store and raise them yourself. If this is your first time, you'll want to organize your "brooder area" and get prepared before they arrive. When your chicks do arrive, you'll need to have a setup that provides a warm, dry, draft-free, clean, escape-proof, safe place to live.

The brooder can be a cardboard box, a large Rubbermaid container (keep the plastic lid that comes with it off), a wire cage with *very* small holes and the sides covered to prevent drafts, or a new or clean and sanitized livestock trough. Cover the top of the container if it's open with something like wire mesh because baby chicks can flutter and fly right over the top and quickly get chilled and die or become lunch for a predator (perhaps even a pet).

You can buy packaged litter or you can make your own by tearing up newspaper and adding that to the bottom of the brooder. Hay and pine shavings work well also. Straw and layers of unshredded newspaper can be slippery and cause the chicks' legs to permanently grow at an angle, and they won't be able to walk properly. You'll notice that, at first, the chicks will peck at the litter as much as at their food. They're not good at distinguishing between what is and what isn't food, so keep their litter clean.

You'll also need a good thermometer to help you regulate the temperature in the brooder.

Invest in a special brooder light with an infrared bulb—regular bulbs are too bright and can cause the chicks to peck each other (which sometimes happens anyway), and it's hard to get the right temperature with them. Brooder lights also have safety features that will keep them from igniting the litter if they fall or tip over. Maintain a temperature of between 90 and 100 degrees for the first week and then start lowering the temperature 5 degrees every week by moving the light up (or the brooder down), until the thermometer registers about 70 degrees. By this time, the chicks should be ready to go outside at least during the day unless the weather is still cool.

Now, buy the chicks! Place them in the brooder with the heat source already on and the area warmed up to about 95 degrees in the heat zone. (It can be a bit cooler around the edges, so they can get away from the heat for short periods.) Make sure they get the hang of taking a drink first thing. You can do this by sticking their beaks into the water container several times. They should catch on fairly quickly, but if there are any chicks that seem to be slow learners, separate them and work with them gently until they drink. Remember that baby chicks can easily drown in their water containers (turkeys are even more prone to this), so don't use water dishes designed for adult chickens. Also make sure that the water dish is stable and won't overturn. Baby chicks don't know enough to stay out of the wet area, and they will get chilled quickly. Chicks drink way more than they eat, so check often to make sure they have access to plenty of clean water. Use tepid water versus cold, and keep their feeding areas away from the heat source.

Next, you'll want to observe the chicks to make sure they're pecking their starter feed. Baby chicks automatically peck at the ground, but they don't always know what food is, so keep it at ground level and easy to get to. They will also poop in their feeders so keep this in mind when you're arranging things. Check the feeders often to make sure the food is staying clean. I generally keep two rotations going, and provide them with a bit less food, but rotate often. When I place the new batch of food into the brooder, I take away the old one and give it a good cleaning, making sure it's absolutely dry before I place more food into it.

Once the chicks are about a week old, you can tell if they are too hot or too cold, but until then, rely on the thermometer. They'll either bunch up together in the warmest part of the brooder if they're cold, or they will get as far away from the heat source as they can and possibly even pant if too warm. Adjust their heat source until they appear content. During the first several days especially, it's a good idea to check on them often, including two or three times during the night.

Common Health Problems for Chickens

Newborn chicks are really quite hardy if they are kept warm and their area is kept clean. It's fun to watch them race around cheeping and pecking and fluttering their tiny wings. But things do happen, and you'll want to stay on top of the situation so you can quickly head off problems.

Diarrhea. Sometimes baby chicks will develop diarrhea, but you can do a lot toward keeping this at bay. Good management practices are your best defense against diarrhea. Don't crowd the chickens, keep their litter clean and dry, and always make sure their food and water containers are clean. I scrub the containers daily, but sterilizing them once a week is a good option also. You can add one tablespoon of regular white vinegar to each quart of drinking water as a homemade remedy for diarrhea, and there are also medicated chick feeds you can buy. If you notice a sick chick, separate it from the rest of the flock and give it special attention until the diarrhea is taken care of.

Pasted vents. Sometimes the chicks' bottoms will get clogged with dried poop. This must be taken care of immediately. Take a warm, wet, soft cloth (old cloth diapers or baby washcloths work well. Don't use paper towels) and gently clean their bottoms. It will take some doing, but stay with it until they are cleaned up. Don't rub hard because their baby fluff will come off, and you can rub their skin raw in a hurry. Some of their fluff will probably come off no matter how careful you are, but *gently* persevere until they are thoroughly cleaned. Put some Vaseline on the area and get the chick warm and dry before placing it back in with its littermates. Watch carefully to make sure the other chicks don't start pecking the raw area.

Pecking each other. Sometimes chicks (and adult chickens) will peck at each other or, more likely, choose one particular chick to concentrate on. Thickly slather on Vaseline to the affected area, and if possible, separate the picked-on bird for a time. I've only had this happen once, and I never could figure out why it started up. There are a number of generally accepted reasons why this can happen: the lights are too bright in the brooder area (hence the use of special brooder lightbulbs), overcrowding, poor diet, inadequate feeder or water container space for the number of birds, or establishing the "pecking order" in the flock.

Diet

The easiest way to give your chickens a balanced diet is to buy commercial feed. You start with "chick" starter in a "crumbles" form, and then move to a "grower" ration, and finally to a "layer" mix. This is also the most expensive route, and these feeds will often have medications that you may not want to include in your chickens' diet. You can choose instead to buy *organic* chicken rations, but these are even more expensive. If you're raising just a few backyard layers, and they are confined most of the time, commercial feed will help keep your hens healthy, which means they'll lay lots of good-tasting eggs for you.

You can make your own feed instead of buying it, but that takes some serious research and mixing to get a healthy ration. There are lots of strong, differing opinions as to what is and isn't good for chickens, so be careful when choosing to mix your own chicken feed.

Even if you choose to feed your flock a commercial mix, you'll still want to give them added greens. These can be grass, weeds, garden residue such as pulled up vegetable plants, and kitchen scraps. Chickens also like meat, and they will benefit from the added protein in their diet if you give them *fresh* (not rancid) meat scraps now and again. Other sources of protein include milk, yogurt, cottage cheese, and even canned cat food. And don't forget bugs and worms. Chickens love them! You can lay out boards in your garden area and then lift them up in the morning to see what's wiggling and crawling underneath. Whatever bugs are there, throw them into the chicken pen and give your hens a special treat.

You'll also need to provide your chickens with a form of calcium, such as ground oyster shells. Many people will tell you that you can give your chickens crushed eggshells that have been dried (try baking them on low heat in your oven), but I never do this because I don't want them to develop a taste for eggshells and start eating their own eggs. (Once chickens become egg eaters, about the only cure I've found is to throw them into the stew pot.)

You'll also want to give them grit for their gizzards. When they're babies, use a small amount of sand and then use larger grit (they pick up small pebbles for this purpose if they're free range) as they get bigger. You can buy grit or if you let them roam free they'll pick up grit from scratching in the yard. Chickens have no teeth (that's where we get the expression "rare as hens' teeth"), and they use grit in their gizzards to pulverize grains and seeds before digesting.

Ensuring that your chickens eat properly for maximum nutrition and health may seem daunting, but just remember these few essentials:

- Provide food at all times. Refill containers when they're almost empty because you don't want feed to get old and turn rancid.

- Regularly give chickens treats and extras in the form of protein, scratch (corn is a favorite), and greens.

- Chickens need a steady source of fresh, clean water, and they will drink a surprising amount, especially in hot weather. In very cold weather, provide warm water for them several times a day if possible, and make sure their water doesn't freeze.

- Keep a dish of crushed oyster shells on hand for their calcium needs. Calcium makes strong bones for the chickens and thick shells for the eggs.
- Provide grit if your chickens are always cooped.
- Periodically clean and sanitize their food and water containers.

Housing

Chicken houses come in all shapes and sizes. Some chickens spend their entire lives indoors, while in other flocks the chickens rarely go inside except to lay eggs and sleep at night. In an ideal chicken coop setup, there will be a henhouse and an outside area where the chickens can run around, scratch, and peck at the ground.

The Henhouse

There are well-designed and beautiful henhouses for sale today, but you can provide great chicken accommodations without spending a lot of money. If you choose to build your own coop, keep these concerns in mind.

Size. You'll need approximately two square feet of space for each chicken, unless they'll be fully confined, in which case you'll need at least double that square footage. You'll also need more room if you choose to feed them inside the henhouse.

Flooring. Cement is the longest-lasting and most easily cleaned flooring, but it's also expensive and hard to install. And if you plan on having a movable henhouse and coop (often called "chicken tractors"), cement floors won't be at all practical. Dirt is fine, but you'll need to provide plenty of litter in the form of hay or other organic material, especially during wet weather, so the chickens won't pick up diseases or parasites from muddy ground. If you utilize the moving "chicken tractor" system, you'll need to move the chickens to a new spot before their current space has been turned to dirt. You want to leave some vegetation anyway so the area will regrow and be ready for the next time the chickens visit. Wood floors are also used, but these tend to rot and smell over time, and they can be difficult to clean. Wood floors are a good choice if you plan on raising the henhouse floor above the ground. Being off the ground lets the wood dry out from underneath.

Light. Windows placed on the sun side of the henhouse (the south side in the northern hemisphere) will let in natural light. You can also add electric lights if the henhouse is wired for electricity. The amount of light in a day affects your chickens' egg laying, so you'll want to maximize their exposure to light. If you provide artificial light, your chickens will continue to lay even during the short days of winter. They do need sleep to stay healthy, so don't leave the light on all the time.

Ventilation. Chickens produce a lot of moisture, both in their breath exhalations and their droppings. If there is insufficient ventilation in the henhouse, ammonia will build up and cause severe health problems as well as "manure burns." Provide ventilation in at least two walls, but during cold weather you can close up all but one window, which should be enough to circulate the moisture and ammonia away from inside but keep cross drafts from chilling the chickens. Make sure the roof overhangs enough above the ventilation areas so driving rain and snow can't enter, but not so low that it blocks the sun.

Insulation. If you live in a cold zone, you'll want to provide some kind of heat in the form of insulation, electric heat, or even a lightbulb or two. When you build the house, build your walls in two layers with some kind of insulation between them.

Nest boxes. One nest box per three or four birds works well. You don't need a nest box for each bird. Nest boxes should be about a foot square, with three sides and a top. One side is left open but with a low lip so the chicken can enter easily to lay her egg. Put straw in the bottom of the box so the eggs have something soft to land on. Make sure the nest bedding isn't higher than the lip of the open side or the eggs could roll out and crack or break. If you slant the roof of the nesting boxes, the chickens won't be as likely to roost on top at night, which will keep the area cleaner.

Roosts. If you provide roosts (a good idea), allow 8 to 12 inches of roosting space for each bird. Place the roosts at least a foot off the ground if possible. Chickens poop a lot while they are roosting, so make sure the roosts aren't placed above nesting boxes or the food and water area. You can make a roost from a tree branch or 2 x 2 lumber. Don't use plastic pipe or other similar materials because they're slippery and the chickens won't be able to cling to them.

Doors. If your henhouse is tall enough for you to enter, you'll need a "person door" so you can go in and out to clean, spread fresh litter, feed, and collect eggs. An even better system for egg collecting is to have an egg door in the wall near the nest boxes so you can simply open it daily to collect all the eggs. In some small backyard coops, the roof is hinged and can be propped open to collect eggs and clean out the house. The chicken door for the henhouse can simply be an opening about a foot square. If you don't have a fenced chicken run, you'll need to have a door that can be closed and latched at night so predators can't get in.

The Coop Yard

The coop yard is where your chickens will spend most of their awake time, pecking, scratching, and exercising. You'll want to have a portion of it in the sunshine and a portion in the shade. Chickens need sunshine to produce vitamin D, and they love a good dust bath during hot weather. The coop yard can also be used to feed and water your chickens, but make sure the feed container won't get rained on and ruin the food. If you build a raised henhouse at one end of your coop, the shade produced under the house can also double as a feeding area. Chickens aren't very good flyers, but they can fly, so it's a good idea to put chicken wire or mesh over the top of the fenced-in yard. An added bonus is that topping the yard area will help keep predators out.

Install a chicken door in the fencing (about a foot square) so you can let your hens in and out. Even if you decide you won't let them range free, you'll need to get them in and out from time to time. If your coop sits in a permanent place and is tall enough for a human to enter, you'll also need a people door so you can go in and out to refill the food and water containers, collect any eggs laid outside nests, and periodically clean out old straw and then strew in fresh. And do use litter. It helps keep the manure smell down and gives the hens something to scratch.

Chicken Tractors

"Chicken tractors" are usually used with small flocks of several chickens, although I've seen one that housed 50 or so hens and was slowly moved with a motorized driver. Chicken tractors are simply henhouses with attached coop yard fencing that often have wheels at one end and handles at the other end. They're made so you can move the entire building, yard, and chickens to a different place. This is a great choice for a small backyard flock of two to six hens. The coop may measure three to four feet wide, and the yard will extend another four to six feet. The construction needs to be sturdy so it won't jiggle apart from being moved often. You also want it built well so predators can't knock it over or tip it up to get at your chickens.

Since I moved to a small town, this is what I currently use. It's working great. The framing construction is 2 x 4s, so it's quite heavy to move around, but I can do it. Because the coop is small, I need to stay on top of the cleaning to avoid chicken manure odors. I let my chickens roam around the backyard on nice days when I'm home and can watch out for them. I'm diligent to move their coop regularly enough that they have new ground to work up.

Chicken tractors are great to put in your vegetable garden at the end of the growing season. The chickens will happily shred the plant wastes and eat any harvest missed or overripe vegetables. They'll till the ground with their scratching and add fertilizer with their droppings. They'll also enjoy any bugs they find. Chickens will generally improve your garden plot. The only caveat is that fresh chicken manure will burn crops, so don't immediately plant an area that has recently played host to chickens.

Eggs

For most of us, the reason we keep chickens is for the eggs. If you've never eaten a homegrown egg, you're in for a treat…and maybe a bit of a shock. Homegrown eggs usually have yolks that are brighter and more intense than store-bought eggs. Sometimes the yolks verge on brilliant orange. The eggs are so much fresher than what you buy in stores, so you'll notice right away that the whites aren't runny and the yolks sit high in the pan.

If you decide to hard boil these incredibly fresh eggs, you might get frustrated quickly when it comes time to peel them. Eggshells don't come off neatly or easily, and bits of the cooked whites will come off with the shell. But if it's egg salad you're wanting to make, or if you're using cut-up, hard-boiled eggs in a recipe such as potato salad, your fresh backyard eggs will be a delight. If the recipe calls for a specific number of hard-boiled eggs, you might want to prepare one or two extra to compensate for the loss of whites when the eggs are peeled. The best idea if you wish to make deviled eggs or have nicely peeled hard-boiled eggs is to use older ones. The longer the eggs have been stored, the easier the shells are to peel off.

Egg Laying and Molting

Modern production chickens have had a lot of their natural tendencies bred out of them, but if you choose to get a heritage breed for your own small flock (and I hope you do!), you'll find your chickens will follow a cycle of egg laying and molting that roughly corresponds with the seasons.

Young hens, called pullets, will begin egg laying when they're 20 to 24 weeks old. At first the eggs will be small and the laying sporadic. But the hens will gradually lay larger eggs and increase their productivity until they are at full production levels, laying 200 to 220 eggs in the first year. Hens will lay 20 percent fewer eggs in their second season, and they continue to lay fewer and fewer eggs each year until they are no longer laying at all, after seven or eight years.

Commercial egg producers usually cull their layers after the first or second season. In a family flock, you can choose to keep your chickens longer. While it's true that a hen will eat the same amount of food whether she's laying or not, backyard chickens can become pets, and many an older hen has happily lived out her days safe from the stew pot. I tend to get attached to my chickens, and when a hen is getting older, I remind myself that she is still producing manure that will get composted and added to my gardens.

During the year, hens will usually lay eggs until they begin their molt, which occurs when the days start getting shorter (the molt is triggered by a decrease in the amount of sunlight the hens experience). In my area, this is usually sometime in early October. Once their molt is complete and new feathers have come in, the hens will start laying again. My hens begin laying again as early as November or as late as February. Bear in mind that different breeds and even individual chickens may vary in molt duration, frequency, and egg laying. Egg production levels may also vary from year to year. For instance, we've just come off a winter here in the Pacific Northwest where many of our flocks never stopped laying. They definitely slowed down, but fresh eggs appeared throughout the entire winter months.

Gathering and Storing Eggs

When a chicken lays an egg, there is a substance called "bloom" that covers the egg. After the egg is laid, the bloom quickly dries into a clear protective coating over the entire shell. This bloom is what helps the eggs stay fresh for long periods, even if they sit around outside or on a counter in the kitchen. So when you gather eggs, don't wash them off unless they are very dirty. Usually a soft, slightly damp cloth will suffice, but if they are muddy or have manure from the chickens on them, it's a good idea to wash them so germs don't migrate into the egg itself. If you do clean them, immediately refrigerate those eggs and use them first because the bloom is now gone and they won't stay fresh as long. They'll still stay fresh for a couple of months as long as they are refrigerated. Some people have good results by rubbing a thin coat of mineral oil over the freshly washed and dried shells and believe the eggs will last for many months if refrigerated.

You don't need to gather eggs more than once a day. In hot weather you might want to gather them more often, but chickens generally lay their eggs in the morning, and usually about the same time each day. If you schedule your egg gathering after they lay, one trip out to the henhouse is all you'll really need to do. But if you can't get to your egg gathering until later in the day, don't worry. Your eggs will be fine. Place the unwashed eggs in empty containers (old egg cartons are perfect for this) and store them in your refrigerator. Wash them when you get ready to use them.

Unwashed, refrigerated eggs can last in the refrigerator for four months or more. If you aren't sure whether an egg is fresh enough to use, place the egg in a bowl of cool water. If it sits on the bottom or if one end slightly rises, it's good. The older an egg gets, the higher that one end will rise. If the egg floats, don't even crack it open because it's rotten. If there's any question about whether an egg is good to use, crack it into a separate container to check before you put it in the mixing bowl or frying pan.

If you have extra eggs you want to keep for when your hens aren't producing, you can freeze them. Break an egg or two into a small bowl, add a tiny pinch of salt or sugar, and gently scramble the egg so the yolk is broken and swirled into the white but isn't full of air bubbles. You can freeze them in muffin pans, and then pop the frozen eggs into a freezer bag or container, or you can pour the liquid eggs into small freezer bags and freeze straightaway. You can also freeze larger amounts of "scrambled" eggs in quantities that you use often. (Just remember to use a larger quantity of salt or sugar to stabilize the eggs.) When ready to use, defrost the eggs in the refrigerator or place the container in a sink filled with tepid water. You can use these thawed scrambled eggs just as you would if they were fresh.

Resources

Because so many people are raising chickens in their backyards these days, you'll find plenty of interesting magazines, books, and websites pertaining to raising chickens. Some of the better ones I've found are:

- www.backyardchickens.com
- www.backyardpoultrymag.com
- www.motherearthnews.com
- Gail Damerow, *Storey's Guide to Raising Chickens* (3rd ed.)
- Carla Emery, *The Encyclopedia of Country Living* (10th ed.)
- Robert and Hannah Litt, *A Chicken in Every Yard*
- Harvey Ussery, *The Small-Scale Poultry Flock*

Bees, Rabbits, and Goats

Bees

There are people in my community who have been quietly raising bees for years, and while their neighbors may not be aware this backyard "livestock" is close by, they are benefiting from that proximity. Bees are essential for pollinating food crops, fruit and nut trees, berry and grape vines, and flowers. Without bees, we'd be hard-pressed to grow food. There are about 4000 different bee species in North America alone, but the bees we usually think of when we consider beekeeping are honeybees. Honeybees aren't native to North America; they were brought over by European settlers several hundred years ago.

You can maintain beehives in suburban backyards or even on urban rooftops, but first research the local ordinances and regulations to make sure it's legal in your area and to find out if there are any special rules. Keeping bees in the city might seem less desirable than keeping bees in the middle of vast swaths of farmland, but in recent years some research has shown that urban and suburban bee colonies are healthier than their rural cousins, possibly due to the heavy use of pesticides and herbicides in commercial growing operations, as well as urban bees having more varied flowering time boundaries versus bees among the typical monoculture practices of commercial growers.

Apart from the initial setup, keeping bees takes minimal work, although harvesting the honey can sometimes be tricky because entire colonies of bees can be wiped out by "colony collapse disorder," pesticide use in nearby areas, and various mites and diseases. Learning how to keep bees takes research, and it's best learned hands-on if at all possible. If you want to keep bees, join a local beekeeping group or find a beekeeper who will let you tag along. Ask questions!

When you provide a beehive for a colony of bees, you won't be able to immediately harvest honey. The bees need to establish their colony and lay in enough honey for their own needs first. What you will be harvesting is their excess—on average about three or four gallons per hive (that's between 36 and 48 *pounds*) per year.

Keep these factors in mind if you want to keep bees:

- Research local ordinances.

- Get good books on keeping bees, and take a beginner's class if one is offered in your area.

- Join a local beekeeper's club. Make friends with someone willing to mentor you.

- Gather your tools and be prepared *before* your bees arrive. You'll need hives, protective clothing, extractor tools, extractor (you may be able to rent this from your local beekeeper's club), and so forth.

- Buy bees that are known to be gentle.

- If your bees will be in a yard, make sure you have fencing surrounding the hive area that is made of wood (no chain-link fences) and is at least higher than a man's head so the bees have to fly up and then out when they are coming and going, otherwise their flight path might place them near people, increasing the potential for stings.

- Tell your neighbors about your beekeeping endeavors. Answer any questions they may have. You might even want to be prepared with a handout that answers typical questions. Share some of your precious honey when you harvest. They'll be grateful.

- Check your hives regularly—at least every week or two—so you can get a head start on any problems.

If you choose to not keep bees but you want to attract these productive pollinators to your garden, here are some things you can do.

- Do not use chemical pesticides on any of your plants. This is very important!

- Plant bee-friendly plants to improve bee habitat in your yard. If you go to a first-rate local nursery, they should be able to help you with what kinds of plants to choose.

- Don't be a compulsive garden tidier. Bees (and other insects) find safe havens around the "wild" edges in your yard.

Colony Collapse Disorder

In late 2006 in North America, reports started coming in that the worker bees in many honeybee colonies were disappearing. Since that time, the phenomenon has been termed "colony collapse disorder." No one knows for sure why this disorder is happening; therefore, there is no consensus on how this can be combated. Studies have also shown that wild colonies of bees have also been affected. If you keep bees, you'll want to stay on top of any research that becomes available on this important topic.

African "Killer Bees"

Africanized "killer bees" started with a beekeeping mistake in Brazil in 1957. The year before, African honeybees were introduced into that country. The idea was to crossbreed them with the established European honeybees that lived in Brazil with the hope that the crossbreeds could better withstand the tropical South American climate. Some of the African honeybees were accidentally released, and they began to establish colonies as they spread northward. The reason these bees are called "killer" is because they are easily irritated and will aggressively defend their territory in large numbers and for longer periods of time than ordinary honeybees. They will pursue a perceived enemy for up to a quarter of a mile. Africanized honeybees have made appearances in the southwestern tier of the United States, and are moving northward with the passing years. If you chance upon a wild swarm of bees, it's best to immediately contact local authorities so it can be disposed of in an appropriate manner, whether that's extermination or catching the swarm and transporting it elsewhere.

Beekeeping Resources

Bees and the keeping of them are mysterious and somewhat intimidating for many people, but there are good reasons to consider going into apiculture. The following resources are a good place to begin.

- www.glorybee.com (located in the Pacific Northwest, excellent products for all beekeepers as well as a large catalog with bulk grains, honey, personal care items, soapmaking and candle-making supplies)
- www.honey.com (the National Honey Board website)
- Howland Blackiston, *Beekeeping for Dummies*
- Lark Crafts, *Homemade Living: Keeping Bees with Ashley English—All You Need to Know to Tend Hives, Harvest Honey & More*
- Kim Flottum, *The Backyard Beekeeper—An Absolute Beginner's Guide to Keeping Bees in Your Yard and Garden*

Rabbits

I've raised a lot of rabbits over the years, in large part because I'm a spinner and knitter and angora rabbit fiber is soft luxury and a joy to work with. But I'll tell you up front that I've only raised meat rabbits one time. Butchering those critters just wasn't something I could comfortably do, although I love rabbit meat. Sometimes I wish I didn't mind the rabbit butchering part, but since I do I content myself with buying rabbits already butchered and put in neat packages at the grocery store.

Raising rabbits for part of your meat source is an excellent choice. One male and female rabbit can easily produce 60 or more offspring in a year. Rabbits are quiet, friendly, and usually docile. And their feed-to-meat ratio is one of the best. Rabbit meat is lean and tasty. Usually even finicky eaters won't balk at eating it—especially if you don't tell them beforehand what's on their plates.

Meat Breeds

The two main meat producers are the New Zealand and California breeds, but there are many more rabbit breeds that come in many sizes, from dwarfs (adults weigh 3 to 4 pounds) up to giants (these monsters can weigh as much as 14 pounds). New Zealands and Californians are in the moderate-sized range, with adults weighing 8 to 12 pounds. The does (females) weigh more than the bucks (males). These rabbits dress out at about three pounds when they are three months old, and more if you let them live a bit longer. Like chickens, rabbits are more tender when they are young. Cook them like you would chicken—fried, roasted, and in stews and casseroles.

Housing

Wire rabbit hutches are the usual housing. They're easy to keep clean and rabbits can't gnaw through the metal like they sometimes do with wood hutches. Wire hutches are either suspended from a ceiling or raised off the ground on legs.

You can also build wooden hutches, but the rabbit urine will soon rot the wood and cause odor problems unless you keep them well cleaned, which is hard to do. The urine-soaked wood can also cause skin burn on the rabbits.

Another housing option is to allow rabbits to live somewhat naturally in a communal, enclosed run area. You'll need to ensure they're safe from predators and have shelter from the worst of the weather, but if you have the room, runs provide your rabbits with exercise and grasses and plants to eat. Keep in mind that you'll need to make the walls of the run at least four feet high so the rabbits can't jump out.

Even if you keep your rabbits in hutches, it's a good idea to allow them to run around your yard during nice days so they can exercise and eat fresh greens. A fenced-in area will keep them from getting into your garden or wandering off. Rabbits do burrow, so make sure that any fencing goes completely down to the ground, and watch them carefully. I've found that as long as the rabbits are happy—that is, they have food, water, and something to keep them occupied and interested—they won't be inclined to burrow their way out of their enclosure.

Weather Considerations

Probably the most important factor when situating your "rabbitry" is making sure the rabbits won't get overheated. Some sun is good for them, but on hot days you'll need to make sure they have lots of ventilation and plenty of shade. It's also a good idea to spray down the hutch roof with water on especially hot afternoons to cool their area.

Rabbits can withstand some cold weather, but during cold winters, you'll need to place boards around the sides of their hutch and wooden skirting under the cage to keep out drafts. Make sure their area is protected from wind. Another option is to move their hutches into an outbuilding or the garage for a snug winter home.

You'll also want to make sure your rabbits are kept dry during rainy weather. This can be easily accomplished by having a roof with overhangs all the way around the cages and possibly solid siding if blowing rain is a problem. Or you can keep your rabbitry under cover in an outbuilding or on a covered patio. Even if you decide on a natural run situation, you'll need to cover the run area so the dirt in the yard area doesn't turn into a muddy mess. You want the rabbits to stay clean and dry.

Predators

Besides the usual predators for small animals, such as birds of prey and coyotes, the most common predators of rabbits are often found in your own or a neighbor's backyard. Dogs and cats kill rabbits. If possible, put up a high and sturdy fence surrounding your rabbitry, and make sure the fencing and hutch roof are strong enough to keep out even the most persistent predator.

Food and Water

Like most animals, rabbits need more water than you might think. Plan on up to a half-gallon of water per day per rabbit, especially in hot weather. They like cool, clean water, so it's best to refresh their drinking containers more than once during the day. When the weather turns cold, you'll need to check that their water containers don't freeze and immediately take care of that problem as it occurs. You can water and feed them at the same time, which is usually once in the morning and once in the afternoon. Especially during hot weather, rabbits will eat more during the nighttime hours than daylight hours. You can give young or nursing does as much food as they want, but when they get older, it's best to feed them limited quantities—about six ounces of feed per day plus all the hay they want.

The easiest way to feed your rabbits is to buy specially formulated rabbit food that comes in the form of pellets at your local feed or pet store. Even if you choose commercial feed, do give your rabbits greens in the form of alfalfa (cut into two-inch lengths), lettuce, grass clippings from your lawn if you don't use chemicals, dandelions, carrots (including the tops), cabbage, and fresh bread soaked in milk. They also enjoy green beans and peas, including the vines, and other grains such as oats and barley. *Do not* give them spinach, potato peelings, Swiss chard, lima beans and vines, rhubarb leaves, or tomato leaves. In fact, because so many common plants can make rabbits sick, it's a good idea to obtain a list of greens they can and can't eat before you give something to them. Also provide them with a mineral/salt block.

Rabbits are chewers, so keep something they can chew on in their hutch. A piece of wood or untreated lumber can provide hours of entertainment. If the containers aren't tied down, rabbits will turn over their food and water bowls and throw them around their cages for something to do. I recommend you give them toys they can play with. I used to give my rabbits small cardboard tubes and fruit tree branches. I've also heard they like straw balls, like the ones you can purchase in the pet sections of stores.

Resources

www.arba.net (American Rabbit Breeders Association)
www.motherearthnews.com (search "rabbits")
www.rabbit.org
Bob Bennett, *Storey's Guide to Raising Rabbits*
Ann Kanable, *Raising Rabbits the Modern Way*

Dairy Goats

I've raised my share of goats, and they were alternately the best and the worst animals on the face of the planet, depending on what they were doing at the moment. My favorite was a Nubian named Jasmine. She was beautiful with her floppy ears (a Nubian trait), liquid-looking eyes, and curious nature. Whenever I was in her pasture, she was sure to find out what I was up to. If I stopped to do something, she'd come up behind me, place her forelegs on my shoulders, and peer around my head for a "goat's eye view." That grinning goat face just inches from my own was always a welcome pleasure. She was a dear. But it's just as true that she got into her share of trouble—a goat trait. Countless times I'd come outside and find her and her sister outside of their pen and wandering through my garden or standing on the hood of my car. They love high places. In fact, goats are the animal that originated the game called "King of the Hill."

It may surprise you that it's entirely possible to raise a couple of milk goats in your backyard even if you live in the city. You can legally raise female goats (does) in San Francisco, Chicago, Seattle, Cleveland, San Diego, and Fort Worth, to name a few forward-thinking cities. In fact, I've heard it said that "backyard goats are the new chickens" when it comes to *the* backyard livestock to own. As with all livestock, however, you'll have to do your research and see what the regulations are in your town.

The first thing is to decide if keeping a couple of goats for your family's milk needs (and possibly meat) is worth the time and effort. Goats are time intensive. For your does to freshen (start producing milk), they need to kid (give birth), which means you'll have another animal or two to deal with. You can raise the kids for replacement stock, butcher them when young and tender to feed your family, sell them, or give them away. But you must do something with them.

For roughly 10 months you'll be required to milk your goats once or twice a day or find someone else to do it for you if you'll be away. That's a hard-and-fast commitment that can't be ignored when inconvenient. And to continue the milk cycle, you'll need to arrange for your doe to meet a buck (male goat). Since keeping bucks in the city or a suburban backyard is extremely ill-advised and almost always illegal, this may be difficult. There are very good reasons for not keeping bucks in suburbia. They are stinky, loud, and aggressive. There are many pluses to owning does. Goat's milk is easier than cow's milk for us to digest, and goat's milk is less likely to cause allergic reactions. If you're lactose intolerant, goat's milk might not be a good alternative for you, but if you're allergic to cow's milk, goat's milk may be just the ticket. Goat's milk is higher in calcium and iron than their bovine cousins' milk. An added bonus is that goats are wonderful entertainment. They are friendly, smart, and curious. Even though dairy goats take more work than some backyard livestock, they can be worth every enjoyable and maddening moment. They'll give you healthy, fresh milk, meat on occasion, and many hours of laughter and pleasant diversion.

Breeds

The six main, standard-sized dairy goat breeds are Alpine, LaMancha, Nubian, Oberhasli, Saanen, and Toggenburgs. For people who have small spaces, the dwarf and miniature goats are the best choice.

Nigerian Dwarf and Pygmy dairy goats are dwarf breeds originating in Africa. The Nigerian Dwarf goat is what people usually associate with dwarf dairy goats. Pygmies are milkers too, but they've been bred to be stockier and larger-boned than the Nigerian Dwarfs. Both of these breeds make great pets and can be walked on a leash. They are also friendly and safe around children, although they can knock a toddler over fairly easily when they get to playing or think a youngster has a treat for them. Be watchful when youngsters are around.

Miniature dairy goats are small-sized crossbreeds that result from a standard-sized doe (one of the six breeds previously mentioned) mated with a Nigerian Dwarf buck. The minis are, in my opinion, your best choice for a small-scale, small-space operation like a suburban backyard. Plus, you'll have a greater choice as to what characteristics you want for your herd. Some people love the floppy-eared beauty and high butterfat content you get from Nubian crosses. Others prefer the placid personalities and high milk output of the Saanens or the classic good looks of the Alpine.

When it's time to choose which goats to purchase, keep these points in mind:

- Buy from an established breeder. You'll probably pay more than if you go to a local sale barn or buy somebody's backyard reject, but the lessened risk of problems will more than outweigh the purchase price. Plus, a breeder will usually keep good records, so you have a better idea of exactly what you're purchasing in terms of milk production, twinning, personality, and overall health and care.

- Buy at least two goats. They are herd animals, so they don't thrive when alone.

- If you buy adult goats, plan to buy from a single herd so they don't pine when removed from their herd mates. You can buy two milkers or a pregnant doe and a wether (castrated male goat) to keep her company. Wethers aren't as aggressive and don't stink like intact bucks do. They also don't produce milk and can no longer produce progeny, so they won't "pay" for their upkeep the same way a doe will. Still, depending on the size of your place, they might make great lawn mowers, and they'll provide the necessary companionship for your milker.

- Buy two weaned kids, and you can all get used to one another as they grow up. By giving them lots of good interaction at a young age, your goats are more likely to be friendly and tame, which will be a plus when you commence to milking them.

- Don't keep a buck! Unless you have plenty of land, good fencing, and a large herd of does, bucks aren't a good idea, even if your area allows you to keep one. Remember, they stink, they're aggressive, and they can be loud. Let somebody else house a buck. Take your does to the buck's place when it's time to breed.

Housing

Like all living creatures, goats need a shelter that allows them to get out of the weather and wind, provides adequate outdoor space, and has good fencing. The goat housing can be a shed with a large opening or even a three-sided structure. Make sure the opening points away from the prevailing winds and rain. The interior space needs to be large enough that the goats can always get out of the rain or snow. For two small goats, an 8 x 10-foot space is adequate. If you have the room, goats often like a sleeping platform. Even a foot off the ground makes them happy. For smaller breeds you can use the largest portable dog house you can find. You can also purchase calf or goat hutches that are made from food-grade plastic. Goat hutches are comparatively expensive, but they work very well. They are designed in such a way that goats can't jump on top of them (which they would love to do).

You will also need to have a covered area where your milking platform is that is big enough to accommodate one goat at a time and you. The best setup I ever used consisted of an enclosed shed area at one end where the goat feed was kept, with the milking platform at the other end that was protected on three sides by walls and an alleyway connected the two. The entire area had a roof and rail sides with gates. Since the alleyway between the shed and milking station was covered, I could keep the area bedded with dry straw, and mud wasn't a problem. There was a gate I could shut once I entered the enclosure. Then I opened the gate on the other side of the alley that opened into the goat pen so I could let them in and out at milking time. There was no electricity in the goat shed, so on dark, winter days I'd bring along a lantern and hang it on a nail high up on the wall so I could see what I was doing. Rustic, but it worked.

Place a deep layer of straw bedding on the floor of your goat shelter so they can stay warm and dry, especially during cold weather. Change the bedding often. If ammonia buildup from urine seems to be an issue, you can sprinkle lime or a specially made enzymatic product under the bedding to keep the smell to a minimum. Remember to place and build the goat shelter in such a way that the goats aren't able to jump onto the top of the structure and then escape over a nearby fence. During hot weather, your goats will need plenty of ventilation, and they probably won't use their shelter except possibly at night and to get out of the sun.

Open Space

Goats need fresh air and sunshine. If you keep two small dairy goats, your outside pen area should be approximately 20 feet on each side. Goats are browsers rather than grazers, so a lawn won't interest them in the same way your vegetable garden, orchard, or shrubs will. If they are confined in a small pen area, you need to let them out on occasion while you're there so you can keep them safe and away from your plants. You can tether them in your yard, or train them to walk on a lead or leash, and take them for walks in your neighborhood. Just make sure when you take them for walks there are no loose dogs roaming the streets because that can lead to disaster in a hurry. Especially during fine weather, goats love being outside. They also love to find high places to stand on, so if you can give them something to jump up on they'll be happy. It can be a large tree branch, a wooden structure you've built especially for their playtime, or the like.

Fencing

Goats have an uncanny ability to find and exploit any weakness in your fencing. So make your fences high enough they can't get a running start and scale over them. If you use wood for your fences, run the slats up and down instead of sideways or they will climb the slats and go over the top. They also like to lean against and stand on their fencing, so it needs to be sturdy. Welded wire fencing, firmly secured to 4 x 6-foot posts at least five feet high should do the trick. Chain link fencing will probably work well, but it's expensive. Squared horse fencing with 4 x 4-inch squares will work as will hog or cattle panels, although you'll need to make sure the holes in the fencing material aren't so big that babies (or even wily adults!) can squeeze through.

Fencing is your most important asset in successfully keeping goats in town. But even with the best fencing, your goats are likely to escape from time to time.

Food and Water

Goats need water, hay, grain, minerals, and salt. The higher quality and more complete regimen you follow translates into healthier goats and more milk in your refrigerator, so don't stint on their food requirements.

Water. Goats must have plenty of fresh water to maintain their rumen function and to guard against urinary tract problems and stones (especially in bucks). Goats will turn up their noses at stale or dirty water, so plan on refreshing their supply twice daily if at all possible or install an automatic watering system. If your winters are extremely cold, you'll need to make sure the water doesn't freeze. You may need to resupply their water more often and provide warm water to help them maintain their body temperature during these times. Goats can drink as much as a half gallon or more of water each day. If there are kids (baby goats) in the pen, make sure the water containers are shallow or made especially for goats so the babies can't fall in and drown (for instance, don't use a bucket). Even though goats require clean water, they aren't necessarily fastidious about keeping their supply clean, so devise a system that allows their water to stay uncontaminated. Automatic watering systems are the nicest and easiest way to go, but they can cost quite a bit.

Hay. Feed your goats a good quality alfalfa hay that is a second or later cutting so the alfalfa is finer-stemmed than first cuttings generally produce. A good quality grass hay or a grass/alfalfa mix can be fed too, but alfalfa has the highest protein content. Put the hay in raised hayracks or a manger with a keyhole or wire opening for their heads so they won't waste as much. Goats can become picky eaters, so don't feed them so much of their favorites that they ignore the less-desirable-but-still-good hay.

Grain. Grain is important for the health of goats, but too much can give them urinary tract stones, which can require a veterinarian's care or even kill them. Don't overfeed your goats grain even when they beg you for more—which they will do! There are specially formulated grain mixes you can buy or you can mix your own. To mix your own, buy dry COB (corn, oats, barley) in bulk. Mix in some hard winter wheat berries and sunflower seeds.

Feed lactating does one to two cups of mixed grain a day. Feed them one cup a day if they aren't lactating. For milkers, pour a tablespoon or two of apple cider vinegar (to prevent mastitis) on the grain before feeding it to them. Many goat owners feed their does grain while they're milking them. The does quickly learn that getting into the milking stanchion means a treat is imminent, so milking becomes an easier task. Wethers and bucks (if you choose to own one) should be fed only half a cup per day. If the goats are foraging or being given greens, put a spoonful of baking soda in their grain ration to help guard against bloat.

Salt and minerals. Buy mineral salt blocks specially formulated for goats. There are also dairy mineral blocks or granules you can give your does in addition to the mineral salt blocks. Your local feed and farm store or university extension service can provide valuable information on the best herd management and feeding practices for goats in your area regarding mineral supplements.

Goats are browsers by nature, and they will appreciate it if you bring them treats or allow them to forage. They will browse on grass and weeds, but they also love vegetables, tree branches, raspberry vines, and rosebushes. You can throw an apple or evergreen branch into their pen and offer them carrot, beet, and turnip greens, lettuce, spinach, cornstalks, melons, and squash. Just remember to gradually add green foods to their diet so their systems have time to adjust. Your goats will also relish treats from the kitchen, such as bread, raisins, peanuts, boxed cereal without sugar, and graham crackers. Don't be surprised if one goat loves a particular food while another goat mouths it and then walks away uninterested.

Predators. Goats run when they are frightened, and neighborhood dogs—or even your own dog—will give chase. Dogs are the most common predator of goats in town, and they will maim or kill one if they catch it. If you live outside the city, coyotes can pose a problem too.

And if your goats are constantly getting out, neighbors might lose their patience and call the police or animal control.

Conclusion

I can't say this enough. Your first and most important task if you decide to keep goats is to build sturdy, escape-proof fencing so your goats stay home and stay safe.

Resources

You can learn a lot about keeping dairy goats from studying books, but you'll do even better if you can establish a relationship with the breeder you bought your goats from. This person can be a wealth of information and help from time to time. Having an experienced goat person nearby isn't always possible, so here are some resources that will help you successfully start raising dairy goats and answer most of your questions:

- www.fiascofarm.com
- www.miniaturedairygoats.com
- Carol Amundson, *How to Raise Goats*
- Jerry Belanger, *Storey's Guide to Raising Dairy Goats: Breeds, Care, Dairying, Marketing* (4th edition)
- *Dairy Goat Journal,* 145 Industrial Drive, Medford, WI 54451, 800-551-5691, www.dairygoatjournal.com
- Gail Luttman, *Raising Milk Goats Successfully*
- *Ruminations* magazine, PO Box 859, Ashburnham, MA 01430, 978-827-1305, www.smallfarmgoat.com, highlights Nigerian Dwarf goats and other miniatures

If you decide to keep goats, you'll no doubt develop such skills as how to milk by hand, trim hooves, administer vaccinations, help in difficult birthings (thankfully these are rare), castrate bucks by banding, debud kids' horns, and deworm your herd.

Goats are worth the learning curve! They are sweet-tempered, independent, highly curious animals that will keep your family and you happily entertained while providing tasty, healthy milk and the makings for yogurt, cheese, and ice cream.

6

Keeping Technology Where You Want It

❖ ❖

Godliness with contentment is great gain.

1 Timothy 6:6

The Amish community's avoidance of technology is probably the most confusing aspect of their lifestyle for many of us. But, in fact, the Amish aren't averse to using technology. Rather, they are slow to accept it, and they thoughtfully, prayerfully, and selectively choose which technologies they will allow into their lives and what the limits of use will be. They reason that modern technologies can easily promote inequality, envy, and competition, and will thus contribute to a breakdown in their families and communities. Further, they believe in living simple lives of contentment without an emphasis on accumulation of possessions.

The Old Order Amish choose not to own cars, but they will hire drivers to take them somewhere if the distance is too far for their horse-and-buggy mode of transportation. They believe that owning a vehicle would erode their close-knit communities by making it easy for their members to travel long distances to shop or visit, rather than stay close to home and build relationships within the community.

Telephones are another technology the Amish use but limit. Instead of having a telephone in each house, several families will go in together and maintain a phone at the end of a farm lane or in a barn or shop nearby to be used as needed to make appointments, call a local store about a needed item, or conduct business. Telephones in the home are viewed as intrusive on family life, and being able to easily pick up a phone to call a neighbor or friend would mean face-to-face time with others would be reduced.

Gas and electricity from local power companies aren't used, but the Amish often use alternative energy in the forms of natural gas, batteries, compressed air, propane, gasoline, wind, solar power, diesel engines, and generators. For instance, they might have a propane refrigerator and stove, a gasoline engine to power the wringer washing machine, windmills or solar panels to move water throughout the farm and provide light for their homes, and pneumatic (compressed air) tools in their businesses. In fact, many people are turning to the Amish to gain insights into their energy independence because they are proof that people can live comfortable lives without connecting to outside power lines.

When it comes to social media, such as televisions, radios, and computers, the Amish are much more wary and generally shun all of them. They strongly believe that by viewing or listening to these devices, they would be tempted to consume more of the world's goods, which would go against the principles of simple living they espouse. After all, the Bible adjures people to "not conform to the pattern of this world" (Romans 12:2).

◆ What the Amish Can Teach Us ◆

The Amish thoughtfully choose which technologies and how much of them they will use. We can do the same, and there's no need to call the power company and request our electricity be turned off or to sell our computers and TVs. What we can do is give serious consideration to what these technologies are bringing into our lives and make decisions based on what we desire for our families and ourselves.

For the Amish, scale or size has much to do with their technology decisions. For them, large-scale businesses have lost the human component. They believe it generates a never-ending push to develop, sell, and consume more of the world's goods. "When is enough, enough?" they ask. We would do well to ask ourselves the same question.

I think we agree that technology per se isn't evil. But our growing dependence and fascination with it can't be healthy. The Amish are living proof that we can live full lives without being constantly connected to technology and its sometimes subtle messages that we need more, we need bigger, and we need better.

Based on a sincere desire to consume less of the world's energy, and to fashion a family unit that practices contentment instead of consumerism, here are some thoughts and ideas that may help you.

Transportation

- Buy a vehicle that uses less gas.
- Consider becoming a one-car family.
- Ride a bicycle to and from your destinations when possible.
- Walk. I recently walked to the grocery store and to our local farmer's market, about two miles round-trip. When I was coming home with several bags, a friend drove by and then stopped and asked if my car was broken and did I need a ride. Yes, you may get a few raised eyebrows, but it's good exercise and pleasant to take in your surroundings at a slow, open-air pace.
- Use public transportation.
- Carpool to work or to shop.
- Combine errands you need to drive to so you make one trip instead of several.
- Designate one day a week to drive into town to do errands.
- Eat locally sourced food when you can. The fuel used to transport out-of-season fruits and vegetables thousands of

miles so you can have peaches in December adds up. Just think, that peach you're eating may have traveled further than you ever have.

Around the House

- Install water-saving devices, such as low-flow showerheads.
- Turn off lights you're not using.
- Lower the heating temperature.
- Lower the thermostat on your water heater.
- Turn off the air conditioner, and use fans instead.
- Keep appliances in top running condition. Clean and replace filters regularly.
- Buy energy-efficient appliances.
- Use compact fluorescent (CFL) lightbulbs.
- Use the sun to your advantage on cold days by opening drapes and blinds. On cold, cloudy days and at night, close them to shut out cold air.
- Close drapes and blinds on hot days to keep the heat out. Your house will stay cooler.
- Wash your clothes and dishes with the coolest water that will successfully do the job.
- Run full loads in your dishwasher or wash dishes by hand. Use a wash tub for washing and rinsing instead of letting the water run.
- Don't leave electrical appliances on standby.
- Use small appliances for small jobs, such as a toaster oven instead of your big one.
- Use a lid when cooking, and match the pot size to the burner size.

- Hang your laundry on a clothesline and let the sun dry them instead of using a clothes dryer.

- Say good-bye to power tools. A push mower always starts, and you'll be getting good exercise in the bargain. Sweep your sidewalks instead of using a blower or water from the hose. Use shovels, rakes, and hoes.

- Water your lawn and plants in the cool of the morning or evening to reduce evaporation. Carefully place your hoses and sprinklers so you aren't watering your driveway and sidewalks. Spot irrigate or use soaker hoses.

- Use candles or lanterns.

- Wrap your water heater in an insulating blanket.

- Find and plug air leaks in your house.

- Keep your refrigerator and freezer full by using jugs of water to fill empty spaces. Less energy is used to keep things cool when the fridge is full.

- Hold a no-energy evening. Light candles or lanterns and play board games, tell stories, sing songs, and enjoy being together as a family.

There are so many ways we can save energy by using less of it and making discerning purchases. See how many ways your family can come up with to save on energy. Get creative, reward good ideas, and then implement the suggestions.

Social Media

I read recently that studies show social media is harder to resist than cigarettes and alcohol—and I can believe it. We've all seen people texting nonstop in public places, even when they're with other people. I find it disquieting when I see two people at a restaurant table, each texting on their cell phones and not talking to each other. And while I agree that computers, cell phones, and other electronic devices can be a boon in certain applications, it's also true that when misused and overused, these same devices disconnect us from a vibrant, "here and now" life.

Another result is that our memory capability is eroded. We no longer have to memorize or remember anything. We can simply Google for what we need or want to know and instantly have numerous answers to our questions. Math is no problem. We whip out a calculator and get the correct answer every time. Want to find out what's going on in a faraway sister's life? No need to write a letter. Just e-mail back and forth to get the latest news.

We are increasingly living unexamined lives as we jump from one thought to the next with the click of a mouse. There is no time or need to stop for reflection. And as for opinions, the mainstream view usually prevails when blogged, Facebooked, tweeted, and texted ad nauseam. The loudest voice wins, whether it's the best choice or not.

So let's consider going against the grain a bit by rethinking our use of social media and practicing discernment when it comes to its use and impact in our lives.

Cell Phones

- Stop texting when you're with other people or in public. And please don't text and drive. That's a deadly combination.

- Cut down on your cell phone minutes and stay within your monthly allotment. Turn off your cell phone when you're at work or with friends and family. If you don't want to turn it off, at least turn your phone to silent. If anybody really needs to get in touch with you, they'll leave a voice mail. Plan to check your voice mail, text messages, and Facebook and Twitter accounts at planned intervals throughout the day instead of whenever your phone signals.

- Resist the temptation to get the latest cell phone that hits the market. Use your phone for two years. Most cell phone providers allow upgrades every two years to a new phone at a deeply discounted price.

- Turn your cell phone off or to silent in the evening. Don't let a ringing phone wake you.

Television

- Don't watch television alone, and don't allow your kids to either. There's no need for an electronic babysitter. Instead, make television watching a family event. Record each person's favorite show, and hold a family viewing night, complete with treats.

- Consider downgrading your satellite or cable channel options. You'll save money and avoid temptation when you have fewer channels to choose from.

- Never leave the TV on for background noise. Plan ahead of time which shows you want to watch and then turn the TV on during those times only. Turn the TV off when your show is over.

- Don't eat meals in front of the TV. Meals are meant to be eaten at a table with family, friends, or your own good company.

Computers

- Only power up your computer when you're using it. Resist the urge to keep it on so you can quickly check for messages whenever you walk by.

- Turn off audible notifications for e-mail, text messages, and Facebook and Twitter posts. That will help you choose when to use the technology instead of having technology tell you it's time to check messages.

- Set a limit on your computer use. Use a timer to stick to your allotted time.

- Keep a log to identify time wasters. Are you visiting certain types of websites, such as home and garden, scrapbooking, do-it-yourself, or even simple living too often? Do you spend hours playing online games or virtual window shopping?

- Consider not having an Internet connection at home. Instead, you can use Wi-Fi connections at your local library, bookstore, or coffee shop. Just remember that Wi-Fi connections aren't secure, so don't send personal or bank information over the Internet from those locales.

- Remind yourself often that the real world is far better than the virtual world. Take up a hobby or develop an interest in something that doesn't involve the use of technology. Keep electronics out of all bedrooms and turn everything off an hour or two before bedtime. Use that time to unwind from the day, visit with your family, and get ready for bed.

- Choose one day each week or month to "unplug" for the entire day. Or choose one electronic device to turn off for that period. If you decide to incorporate Sabbath rest days into your schedule, this would be the perfect time to consider unplugging for the day.

National Day of Unplugging

In 2010, a group formed "#Unplug," www.sabbathmanifesto.org, to explore the notion of slowing down and taking a day of rest based on Genesis 2:2: "By the seventh day God had finished the work he had been doing; so on the seventh day he rested from all his work." Every year since, they have initiated a 24-hour National Day of Unplugging. According to the group's website, in 2012 millions of people were involved, and "cell phone sleeping bags" were available to tuck your cell phones and other small electronic devices in to help resist the urge to use them. The group has made it fun to unplug, and they have a list of 10 principles as well as helpful links for anyone interested in moving away from a constantly hectic life.

If you don't want to join the National Day of Unplugging, you could certainly have an Unplug Day of your own. Involve your family, church, and friends, and make the day special. Join together for a pot-luck meal, take a group hike, or come up with some ideas for making a memorable, low-tech day.

7

Waste Not, Want Not

◆ ◆

*[Ruth] went out, entered a field and began
to glean behind the harvesters.*

RUTH 2:3

During World War II, the expression "use it up, wear it out, make it do, or do without" became a popular rallying cry to live frugally as a way to support the war effort. Victory gardens sprang up all over. Knitted garments were unraveled, and the yarn was used to knit up something new, so the "good" yarn could be used to knit helmet liners, caps, socks, and vests for "our boys over there." Clothing was handed down, patched, or remade to get more use out of the fabric until it was considered too threadbare to use. Reducing, reusing, recycling, and repurposing were definitely in. Nothing was thrown away until every possible use for it had been considered.

After the war, Americans became more prosperous and innovations abounded. The spirit of frugality waned. There was no longer any perceived need for thriftiness. Today we live in a world that flaunts materialism and consumerism. When something stops pleasing us or when we "need" the next new thing, we're quick to dispose of a perfectly good item to move on to the next.

❖ What the Amish Can Teach Us ❖

The Amish didn't need a war effort to spur them on to frugal and practical habits of living. For them, being content and making do is their cultural mind-set. Take horse-drawn farm implements, for example. Until early in the twentieth century, most farmers used horses for farming, but with the advent of tractors, the farming scene changed. Soon the Amish were among the only people using the old-style equipment. The result was that many pieces of used horse-drawn farming equipment were sold at very low prices. Amish farmers snapped up these great deals. They used and repaired this equipment for as long as possible. Today some Amish shops design, manufacture, and refit modern horse-drawn implements.

Amish women are generally well-schooled in the art of frugal living. For them it's their way of life. They grow most of the family's food, buy in bulk what they can't grow themselves, sew much of the family's clothing, and use few if any modern appliances. They wash dishes by hand, hang the laundry on clotheslines to dry, can and dry fruits and vegetables for the winter, and cook and serve their families three square meals each and every day. They enjoy shopping at thrift stores and garage sales because they love a bargain. Compared to most of us, Amish women are much better at distinguishing between need and want, and they aren't as likely to buy on impulse.

Creative Thriftiness

Consuming less and being content is built into the Amish way of life. But if the thought of recycling, reusing, reducing, and repurposing seems intimidating, there are small steps you can take to get headed in the right direction. And once you begin to think creatively about making do with what you have on hand, it can become a fun family project.

To get started, why not try to live as thriftily as you can for one month? Engage the entire family in this endeavor by brainstorming ideas. Or you could go on a spending fast for a week (or longer). Plan to spend no money except on real necessities, such as gas for the car to get to and from work, necessary medications, and other essentials. Keep a journal of your week, and enjoy looking at all the ways you made do and consumed less.

There are countless ways to be thrifty. Searching the Internet, talking to friends, and reading books will give you more ideas than you thought possible. Some of them, such as changing your watering system to make use of gray water to irrigate your yard, might be a bit much for the average family, but deciding to separate and recycle the recyclable materials from your garbage can be done with just a little more effort than it took to throw everything into one trash can.

Does the idea of thrift strike a chord? Would you enjoy integrating new, cost-conscious habits into your life? The first and best thing you can do is change your thinking. You're not "doing without." Instead, you're choosing to live responsibly, and that's a great feeling. And remember, every action causes a reaction, so by consuming less, you're freeing up resources for someone else who may be in desperate need. The Bible tells us, "If anyone has material possessions and sees a brother or sister in need but has no pity on them, how can the love of God be in that person?" (1 John 3:17). You might feel as if your actions don't make a bit of difference in the grand scheme of things, but when many of us are choosing to live responsibly, change becomes possible. So when you're confronted with a choice, remember the old adage: Use it up, wear it out, make it do, or do without. You'll be glad you did.

Use It Up

People waste a lot of food they buy. Add to that the uneaten food at restaurants, the grocery store produce and food items tossed when they near their "use by" dates, and the amount of food we throw out is staggering. So what can we do?

- Plan a weekly (or monthly) menu, and stick to it. When you buy your groceries, you'll know what items you need and how much to make the meals you have planned.

- Grow some of your own food. You'll be more likely to eat what's in the garden if you've fussed over and cared for those plants as they matured.

- Eat at home. The best menu planning in the world means nothing if you regularly grab takeout instead.

- Buy seasonal and sale items. When a food is in season, it's usually less expensive and tastes better. Can, freeze, or dehydrate the excess for the winter.

- Eat those leftovers.

- Use personal care products, such as deodorant, shampoo, cosmetics, toothpaste, and lotions, completely before replacing them. Even if you buy in bulk and have a handy supply stashed in a cupboard, develop the habit of using every last drib and drab before you open up a new container. Cosmetics, especially, seem easy to throw away before they're used up. Buy cosmetics as you need them, and only buy what you'll be able to use in a reasonable amount of time.

- You don't need six different kinds of general-purpose cleaners. Use the suggestions in chapter 3, "Housekeeping Tips."

Wear It Out

Cars, clothing, electronics, and appliances are major items that often get dumped before their time is up.

Cars

The U.S. Department of Transportation notes that today's cars last 13 years and 145,000 miles on average, but many cars last longer than that. Regular maintenance is the key. Take good care of your vehicle, and chances are it will serve you well for many years. If you keep your car for 10 or more years, you'll save big time by having fewer car payments over the course of that period. You'll save even more because your car insurance will decrease as your vehicle ages. It's a good idea to budget $500 to $1000 per year for maintenance, but that's only a few months' worth of car payments that you're no longer paying. And if you keep saving a set amount each month beyond that, you'll be well on the road to being able to plunk down a hefty down payment or pay in full when it comes time to buy your next car.

Clothing

Many of us enjoy shopping and finding that "just right" outfit that is the latest fashion. Instead, consider buying classically tailored clothes that are stylish even after several years. For your clothing to last, you need to take good care of them. Keep them clean and mended. If a button comes off or a hem or seam comes apart, fix it. If you don't know how, this is a great time to learn! That way you won't be tempted to throw clothing out prematurely. Also, if you buy most of your clothes within color "families," you'll be able to mix and match, creating more outfit choices. Sell your gently used clothing at a consignment shop, and buy from that shop with the money you earn.

Electronics

Computers, laptops, monitors, cell phones, televisions, microwaves, printers, and fax machines—as new technology comes along, the list of what's available grows and grows. And when we do purchase a piece of electronic equipment, often within months there's an upgrade available, so we feel we've been left behind if we don't upgrade. Resist the urge!

When you bought your electronic gadget, you were pleased with its performance and considered it good enough. Nothing has changed except your expectations, especially because you are constantly bombarded by the "absolutely have to have it" advertising campaigns designed to make you yearn for something just a bit faster or more powerful.

If you develop the practice of repairing and keeping your electronic gadgets until they stop working, you'll save money because you won't be buying as often. When it's finally time to buy a new item, recycle or donate your old one, and then consider buying a used or refurbished gadget instead of a brand-new machine.

Appliances

My first washer and dryer lasted about 20 years. They were workhorses with no bells and whistles. I needed one repair (on my washer) during that entire time. When I finally bought new appliances, I made sure the new ones were workhorses as well. No need for fancy add-ons for me. I wanted my washer to wash, and my dryer to dry. My hope and expectation are that these appliances will last just as long as the first set. How long do large appliances usually last?

- *Up to 20 years:* air conditioner, oven, range, water heater
- *Up to 15 years:* dryer, freezer, refrigerator, washer
- *Up to 10 years:* dishwasher, microwave

The general rule of thumb is that if your appliance breaks and it will cost half as much to repair it as the cost of a new one, donate or recycle the old appliance and buy new. If your appliance is an older model that you expect to get only a few more years of service out of, buying new is also indicated. Newer models come with Energy Star ratings, so do your homework and get an energy miser. The money you save each month won't offset the cost of a brand-new appliance, but every little bit helps. And do check the ads for good, used appliances or store sales on floor samples or last year's models.

You can help your appliance last longer by changing the hoses before they crack or break, cleaning and replacing filters and ventilation lines, vacuuming condenser coils on cooling units (refrigerator), and keeping the seals around doors clean and tight.

Make It Do

Webster's Dictionary defines "make do" as "to get along or manage with the means at hand." There are many ways to make do: repair instead of replace, resole boots and shoes, reupholster to breathe new life and appeal into older furnishings, mend and patch, substitute ingredients when cooking, borrow seldom-used tools instead of buying them, barter with friends and neighbors, give and receive hand-me-downs.

Do Without

Your dishwasher, clothes dryer, or microwave stops working. What do you do? You could get along without the appliance for a time. Then you can decide if you really need to purchase a new one. You might be surprised to find that you don't really miss some items. You really can get by without a microwave or automatic dishwasher. Still, that's a lot to ask of most of us, but when we have an attitude of contentment with our current possessions and learn to no longer be controlled by materialism, consumption, and easy disposability of goods, we free ourselves from the tyranny of "stuff." And the fewer things we own, the less we'll have to organize, clean, repair, replace, and maintain. Not a bad trade-off.

Waste Not, Want Not

Your family may have experienced a job loss or reduction in wages or a large, unexpected expense that will take some time to recover from. Or perhaps you're feeling the effects of the current economic downturn because prices are increasing faster than you can keep up with them. Maybe you have children, and your little ones need to be fed, clothed, and cared for so your budget is strained. Or possibly you're getting closer to the retirement years and realize you need to spend less now to save more for the future.

At the end of the month, if you can consistently spend less than you make, you'll be headed in the right direction. Even if that means just five dollars set aside for a "rainy day," pat yourself on the back because you're five dollars closer to having the funds you just might urgently need someday.

Whatever your reasons for wanting to make changes, the possibilities are almost endless. Here are some ideas for living thriftily and saving money.

- If you spend less, you'll need to earn less, which means you'll have more time to spend with your family and work on meaningful activities.

- Pay off unsecured debt as quickly as is feasible. The most common unsecured debts are from credit cards and personal loans. When you pay off your credit cards, don't keep them in your wallet. This will help you avoid using them for nonessential purchases. Use them only when necessary, and pay them off as quickly as possible.

- To the greatest extent possible, shun all types of debt. Yes, many of us have car loans and home mortgages we're working toward paying off. If you have to borrow, don't borrow the maximum you're able to. Instead, lower your sights a bit. You'll be less stressed each month at bill-paying time when you aren't as strapped for cash as you would be if you were borrowing up to your limit.

- Pay with cash as much as possible.

- Consider taking vacations closer to home to save on travel expenses. Or stay home for your vacation, and explore the sights around your community by taking several day trips instead.

- Take some do-it-yourself (DIY) classes at your local YMCA, community center, library, community college, extension office, or city recreation services. Have you always wanted to know how to change the oil in your car? Or find out how to make candles or homemade bar soap? Or prepare applesauce from the apples on your own trees? Take a class! If you have access to a computer and the Internet, go to www.pinterest.com. There you'll find endless ideas for gardening, food, home decorating, DIY crafts and repairs, and lots more.

- Buy used when appropriate. Discover the joys of going to garage sales, estate sales, second-hand stores, and thrift stores.

- Contact your local garbage service to find out what they accept as recyclable materials. Then have a family meeting to discuss the particulars so everyone knows what to do.

- Walk whenever possible. If a store is within walking distance and you don't have a lot to buy, take a canvas tote or small backpack to pack your groceries in and enjoy the exercise of walking. You'll save on gas and wear and tear on your car, and you won't be tempted to buy more than you planned because you have to cart it home.

- Forget the plastic sandwich and freezer bags. Wash and reuse glass jars with tight-fitting lids. Use canning jars. You can buy plastic screwtop lids made especially for them. Use glass containers of all kinds for saving leftover food and for packing your lunch.

- Pack a lunch if you'll be gone during the day. Include a thermos with coffee, tea, or juice. Your lunch hour will be restful and relaxing if you can stay where you are to eat instead of racing to a restaurant or fast-food joint and standing in line with everyone else.

- Use old clothes for cleaning rags instead of paper towels or disposable cleaning cloths. T-shirts, old kitchen towels, and diapers are best.

- Use cloth napkins instead of paper ones. If they don't get dirty, reuse them before washing. For years our family used slightly damp washcloths for our napkins. They were cheap and lasted a good long while.

- Grow your own food.

- Make garden labels for your plants out of plastic food containers. Cut them in long strips and write with a grease pen or indelible marker.

- When seed starting, use empty, clean yogurt, cottage cheese, and milk containers for pots. Be sure to poke drainage holes in the bottom.

- During dry weather, hang your laundry on a clothesline. They really do smell sweeter when dried on a line. If there's no breeze, some of your laundry may be stiff when dry. Just give them a good shake when you put them up on the line and again when you take them off. That will help. Occasionally I throw the sun-dried laundry into the dryer for five minutes to soften them up.

- Wash dishes by hand. Use a dishpan for the soapy water, and another dishpan for the rinse water instead of letting the faucet run.

- Consider investing in a rotary lawn mower. They have improved greatly over the years, and if you keep the blades sharpened, you'll be able to cut the grass fairly effortlessly.

- Make birthday and holiday gifts.

- Set a limit on the number and cost of gifts you give and receive.

- De-clutter. Sell what you can do without.

- Instead of subscribing to satellite or cable television, buy an antenna.

- Go to the library for good books, movies, and free Internet connections.

- If you're single, consider getting a like-minded roommate. You'll not only share the monthly expenses, but you'll have companionship and a ready-made partner for home maintenance and other projects.

- Observe the "one week rule." Don't buy any nonessential item until you've thought about it for at least a week. Sometimes in the heat of the moment we impulse buy and live to regret it.

- Don't buy individual, plastic-bottled drinking water. Use reusable water bottles and fill them up at home or at work.

- Eat less meat. Good protein alternatives include dry beans, soy products, whey, milk, cottage cheese, hard cheese, whole eggs, canned tuna, Greek yogurt (more protein than regular yogurt), and peanut butter. Include several meatless dinners each week to save money.

- Regarding dry beans—pressure can them for instant meal prep or cook a large batch and freeze in meal-sized portions for later use.

- Buy items in bulk.

- Make your own mixes for everything from biscuits to cake mixes. (Check out my *Homestyle Amish Kitchen Cookbook* for lots of mix-ahead, large-batch recipes.)

- Decrease consumption of convenience foods. Instead, cook from scratch.

- Use coupons, but only for items you normally buy.

- Cancel subscriptions. Magazines are a particular weakness of mine, and I thought I couldn't live happily with less in this area. But even so, I decided to cancel all but one subscription, and I'm perfectly content with this arrangement. I can go to the library for some of my reading, and occasionally I borrow a magazine from a friend to read.

- Telecommute if possible.

- Plan ahead and stay organized so you don't have to spend more for last-minute gifts or ingredients.

- Give up your gym membership. Get your exercise by indulging in an active lifestyle. Clean your house regularly, knead loaves of bread by hand, carry buckets of water and feed to your chickens and goats, and turn over the soil in your vegetable garden with a shovel. You'll never miss the fitness center.

Being thrifty is more a mind-set than a list of actions you follow to reduce your outlay each month. Remember, it's your money. When you decide to take control of your expenditures, you'll find the freedom that comes from an orderly life. Stress is reduced when you aren't constantly shelling out money to pay interest on credit cards and wondering how you'll pay all your bills this month. Having a bit of savings tucked away will be a comforting guard against unexpected needs that pop up from time to time. Saving money also allows you the pleasure of being generous and helping others when you see their needs. Peace will fill your home.

8

Coming Home

◆ ◆

Godliness with contentment is great gain.

1 Timothy 6:6

The question might well be asked, Why would someone wish to embark on a simpler lifestyle when we can get by so easily with ready-made everything? What could possibly be the appeal of such a life where we willingly do chores that aren't necessary for survival; grow, harvest, and preserve a large garden to feed our family when the grocery store is just minutes away by car; and keep milk goats and chickens when we can buy milk and eggs?

Here again, the Amish teach us by their actions. We notice their qualities of industriousness, family connectedness, faith in action, and service to their community, and we wish for the same characteristics. But our hectic schedules mean that we're often tired and overwhelmed by our to-do lists. Who of us wouldn't want to slow down and really savor each moment instead of feeling the need to continually rush around getting it all done?

I don't presume to have answers to *why* you and your family would like to step back and practice simplicity in living, but I *can* share with you some of the reasons my family has lived like this, and the benefits we've realized from our plain and simple life. And maybe some of what we've learned over the years will encourage you to step away from the mad rush of modern life to gain something much deeper.

Reasons for Living a Simple Life

Increasingly, life seems to not be working well for us. The Center for Disease Control reports that 1 in 10 Americans are depressed. According to a March 2012 CBSNews.com special report, rates of depression have been going up over the last several decades in most industrialized nations and have roughly tripled in the last two decades. Add to that the tough economic times and high unemployment rates we're currently experiencing, and it becomes pretty easy to hope there's a different and better way to exist.

Life as we know it is complicated. We must work to provide for our material needs, so every day we consider what we can purchase with our income. Then again, we don't want to focus on materialism. And it takes conviction to stand against the tide and live a different way than the majority, to turn away from some of what this world offers and what our friends and neighbors are working so hard to acquire.

We're sure to get a few odd looks if we decide to tear out our lawns to put in a garden or choose to have chickens clucking in our backyards. On the flip side, some people might become interested in what we're doing. They'll ask questions, and we can help them discover the joy of a simpler life spent worshipping and serving Jesus.

Getting Our Priorities in Order

If we were to list the most important things in life, it's doubtful that material possessions would top that list. Instead, we would probably list intangibles like "more time with my family," "a meaningful ministry," or even "regular, guilt-free time for myself." By prioritizing, we will have the ability to fashion the kind of satisfying life that addresses what's important to us and gives us a sense of purpose.

Something that helped my family was to ask ourselves this question: What is our purpose in life? The Bible tells us that we are created in God's image, and we are to glorify Him in all we do (Genesis 1:27; Isaiah 32:8; 1 Corinthians 10:31). As we studied Jesus' life, it became clear that when our Savior walked the earth, He taught compassion, love, and service to others. By developing the habit of asking ourselves what Jesus would do in our situation, it became easier to point our decisions in the direction of His example.

Our family life was another winner when we set priorities. "God sets the lonely in families" (Psalm 68:6). This was our encouragement to give our family the best of what we had to offer in terms of time and energy and to develop good relationships with those around us. Spending time with family and church folks was our primary entertainment. We indulged in plenty of potlucks and barbecues, Bible studies, and impromptu music fests, where everyone joined in by playing an instrument or singing. We picked berries together and jointly canned the fruit. We shared recipes and clothing patterns, and we cleaned a friend's house or brought dinner when someone was sick or injured.

We have many wonderful memories that were built over the years as a result of those everyday activities. What we lacked in the world's goods was more than made up for by the richness of our connections. And those connections continue to this day. We feel very wealthy by having these wonderful, meaningful relationships.

The Gift of Time

One of the best surprises for us was the gift of time that resulted from our close-to-home lifestyle. By making the decision to make our home the center of our days, we enjoyed plenty of time together. Each day had the potential and power to be memorable and special. My boys had a good time helping their dad build a hog pen or assisting me by "skating" on wet rags to clean the kitchen floor. While it's true we could have done those jobs faster without their help, we would have missed all the fun that came with working together.

When we free up time in our day, we get to fill those hours with whatever suits our interests. We can volunteer our time and skills where they're needed, or we can pursue meaningful hobbies. We can tinker on projects, go for a hike, or sit in the sun and read a great book we've been meaning to get to. And if we have kids at home, we can help them pursue their budding interests. Time is precious! We need to choose how we use it well.

Reduce Stress

First Timothy 6:10 tells us that "the love of money is a root of all kinds of evil. Some people, eager for money, have wandered from the faith and pierced themselves with many griefs." When we choose to eschew some of life's extravagances, we'll find some of our stress melting away. We won't spend as much time fretting about making ends meet because our ends are closer together. When we don't have to work so hard, we'll be more relaxed and refreshed, allowing us better interactions with the people we come into contact with. Deciding to live with less stuff also means those possessions won't be demanding our constant attention to use it, clean it, maintain it, or pay for it.

I live near a highway that goes to the coast, and I often see caravans of travelers with their big new trucks, campers, motorcycles, quads, and boats wending their way west for a few days of play. What always strikes me is how much money is tied up in all those expensive toys. And I'd wager that most of what I see thundering down that highway isn't paid for yet. I'm saddened when I think of all those people enslaved by their possessions. I get frustrated when I think about the better ways their time and money could be utilized.

So far I've not had the urge to want some of those things for myself, but I figure that if I ever do, I can rent a camper for a week and return it when I'm done instead of making a monthly payment for years. That would cost me much less in the long run in terms of time as well as money.

Appreciate What You Have

Have you ever gone into a store with a short, mental list of the items you need and yet found yourself at the checkout counter with a full cart? It happens to us all now and again. Buying something that wasn't on your list isn't necessarily a bad thing, but those unintentional purchases can add up. Becoming aware of those little luxuries and extras will help you become a more thoughtful consumer. It will also give you a greater appreciation for what you already have.

When we satisfy every whim and desire, that abundance makes it easy to forget that all we have comes from God's hand. We run the risk of believing that it's *our* hands that have produced or provided our abundance. And when we think our wealth is due to our own efforts, we could easily become guilty of believing that those who lack resources have brought that upon themselves. The Bible tells us otherwise: "The LORD sends poverty and wealth; he humbles and he exalts" (1 Samuel 2:7).

In our family, we learned the important lesson that what we have has nothing to do with our worth. We worked to meet our needs, and our goal was well-being, not making money or having more possessions. And because we weren't in the habit of always wanting something new, we weren't as distracted by possessions.

Confidence

One of the best bonuses we received from embracing a simple life occurred in the area of our sense of confidence. When we learned how to care for animals, tend a large garden, and repair whatever needed fixing, we soon realized that we were in a much better position to care for our family in the event of a disaster or even day to day. That self-assurance translated into more peaceful days for us.

Stewardship

The Greek word for stewardship is *oikonomos,* which means "household management." Psalm 24:1 states, "The earth is the LORD's, and everything in it, the world, and all who live in it." So as we manage our households, we're really managing what belongs to the Lord. We are responsible for the Lord's resources that have been entrusted to our care.

Now, if what we produce is really God's, then it stands to reason that we can be generous with His supply and give freely and joyfully to those in need. After all, it's not as if God will ever run short. Our task is to be good stewards of His stores, sharing with those in need and being grateful for what we are blessed to have.

Spiritual Blessings

Something our family noticed after embracing the simple life was that we felt closer to God when we were caring for our animals and tending the garden. When our family was young, there was an expression in our Christian circle that went like this: "Be in the world but not of it." We took that to mean many things, one of which was to refashion our home life so we could separate ourselves from the rush and hurry of modern culture. We *didn't* take that to mean that we should head for the hills and become hermits. In fact, quite the opposite. We hoped to be lights that shone in such a way that people would want to know what compelled us to live the way we did. And we found that living our lives locally has allowed us to get to know our neighbors and, in turn, be known by them.

There were other spiritual blessings that came from living this way too. As we went about the business of caring for our bit of land, we developed contemplative spirits because we noticed again and again the providential hand of God. The rains came in season, the winds held off, and the birds sang their sweet songs. But even when things went wrong—when we lost animals or the weather was harsh and we had a crop failure, God's hand could be seen as He provided for us in other, often unexpected ways. And because we chose to live this way, we experienced the blessings that came from being content.

Even though I advocate rural living as a best-case arrangement, I would be wrong to suggest that this is the only way to be close to God. Agrarianism does not equate to godly or simple living. Indeed, I am currently living in town, but I still keep a large garden and raise a few chickens. We can draw close to God wherever and however we choose to live. And I, for one, am grateful that our Lord can be found by all who diligently seek Him, for He is a holy and loving God who patiently waits for us to turn away from sin, "not wanting anyone to perish, but everyone to come to repentance" (2 Peter 3:9).

My Prayer for You

May you be one who has accepted God, "who has called you into fellowship with his Son, Jesus Christ our Lord" (1 Corinthians 1:9). Joy is sure to follow.

◆ ◆ ◆ ◆ ◆

Have I not commanded you?
Be strong and courageous.
Do not be afraid; do not be discouraged,
For the LORD your God will be with you wherever you go.
Joshua 1:9

Recommended Resources

Anabaptist Bookstore
875 N. Pacific Hwy.
Woodburn, OR 97071
www.anabaptistbooks.com

This bookstore has an excellent website that carries many resources from Amish and Conservative Mennonite publishers—many of whom do not have a web presence. There are books on family and marriage, victorious living, youth and adult fiction, Bibles and study aids, and the complete education curriculum from Rod and Staff and Christian Light publishers. There are also a cappella music tapes and CDs for sale featuring Mennonite quartets, quintets, and choirs.

The Budget
PO Box 249
Sugarcreek, OH 44681
330-852-4634
www.thebudgetnewspaper.com

Known as the "Amish Newspaper," *The Budget* has been around since 1890. The national edition, published weekly, is filled with letters sent in by Amish and Mennonite "scribes" who relay the news of interest from their communities. Because telephones aren't part of everyday life for many Amish families, *The Budget* is a handy way to keep abreast of events in surrounding and sometimes far-flung communities where they often have extended family. Even if you're not Amish or Mennonite, *The Budget* is good reading.

Chupp's Herbs & Fabrics
27539 Londick Road
Burr Oak, MI 49030
269-659-3950

Chupp's sells dietary supplements, shoes, fabrics, Mutza suits (men's Amish suits), hats, gloves, toys and games, wagons, hand-powered small kitchen appliances, and more. You can call or write for a free catalog. More than 100 pages are jam-packed with products and testimonials, many from satisfied Amish customers. Makes for interesting reading.

Gohn Brothers
PO Box 1110
105 S. Main Street
Middlebury, IN 46540
800-595-0031
www.gohnbrothers.com

Gohn Brothers has been around for more than 100 years. It sells Amish and Plain clothing and footwear (including old-fashioned, high-topped shoes), books and games, sewing and quilting fabric, sewing accessories, and black Amish bonnets. You can call or write to ask for their free catalog.

Lehman's
One Lehman Circle
PO Box 270
Kidron, OH 44636
888-438-5346
www.lehmans.com

Lehman's supplies the Amish and others with a wide variety of items for people who live without electricity or prefer a self-sufficient lifestyle. You can ask for a catalog to be sent to your home for a small fee (it's worth the price) or you can go online to browse and shop. Lehman's has about everything you could wish for—lanterns (including a large selection of Aladdin lamps and replacement parts), nonelectric kitchen appliances and gadgets, canning utensils, barn and farm supplies, wood-burning cookstoves, propane refrigerators, washday supplies, treadle sewing machines, furniture, toys, and garden implements. If you can think of it, they probably have it or have access to a supplier.

Mennonite Relief Sales
Mennonite Central Committee
704 Main Street
PO Box 500
Akron, PA 17501

You can contact the Mennonite Central Committee (MCC) for a current listing of Mennonite Relief Sales that are held annually in most states and Canadian provinces. While this is not specifically Amish, the Mennonite Relief Sales are so much fun to attend that it's worth going to at least once if there is one near your area. The sales are organized locally by volunteers from Mennonite and Brethren in Christ churches, so each location has its own flavor. Begun in the 1950s, the Relief Sales are designed to raise money to help the less fortunate throughout the world.

You will find many items for sale, including beautiful, handmade quilts, which the Relief Sales are especially known for, as well as furniture, needlework, pottery, woodwork, and paintings. Antiques and other quality used items are also sold. And then there's the food! Thousands of pies, cookies, cakes, breads, and rolls are baked. Home-preserved jams, jellies, pickles, and relishes line the food booths.

The proceeds are donated directly to the Mennonite Central Committee, which uses the funds to provide food and other necessities to war-torn or famine-stricken areas around the globe. Many thousands of visitors attend the Relief Sales each year. It's a good time for a good cause.

Websites for Plain Dress and Coverings

http://www.anabaptistbooks.com/services/sewing (made-to-order dresses)

www.gehmanscountryfabrics.com (fabric and modest clothing)

www.katiesmercantile.com (ready-made, modest clothing)

www.mennonitemaiden.com (clothing patterns and coverings)

www.modestpatterns.com (great clothing patterns)

www.plainlydressed.com (men's and women's plain clothing, coverings, and more)

www.prayercoverings.com

www.quakerjane.com (great website for all things plain)

About the Author

Georgia Varozza, author of *The Homestyle Amish Kitchen Cookbook* (nearly 50,000 copies sold), is a certified master food preserver. She teaches people how to prepare and preserve healthy foods; live simply with integrity, and get the most from what they have. She works in publishing and lives in a small Oregon community. Georgia loves being with her kids and grandkids and enjoys cooking, spinning, and knitting. www.georgiaplainandsimple.blogspot.com

For a taste of Amish cooking, try this!

The Homestyle Amish Kitchen Cookbook: Plainly Delicious Recipes from the Simple Life

by Georgia Varozza

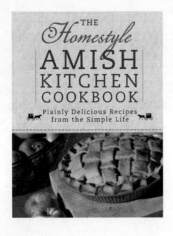

Just about everyone is fascinated by the Amish—their simple faith- and family-centered lifestyle, colorful quilts, and hearty, homemade meals. Straight from the heart of Amish country, this celebration of hearth and home will delight you with the pleasures of the family table as you take a peek at the Amish way of life—a life of self-reliance and peace of mind that many of us long for.

You'll appreciate the tasty, easy-to-prepare recipes that include Scrapple, Graham Nuts Cereal, Potato Rivvel Soup, Amish Dressing, and Snitz Pie. At the same time, you'll learn a bit about the Amish, savor interesting tidbits in the "Amish Kitchen Wisdom" sections, and find out just how much food it takes to feed the large number of folks attending preaching services, barn raisings, weddings, and work frolics.

The Homestyle Amish Kitchen Cookbook is filled with good, old-fashioned family meal ideas to help bring the simple life home.

◆ ◆ ◆ ◆ ◆

Be sure to check out
Harvest House Publishers' Amish Readers' webpage!
www.amishreader.com

More Amish Reading to Brighten Your Day

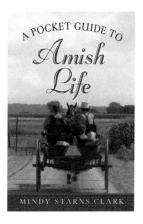

A Pocket Guide to Amish Life
Mindy Starns Clark

You'll enjoy this glimpse into the fascinating world of the Amish—what many of them believe and how they live. Full of fun and fresh facts about the people who abide by this often-misunderstood faith and unique culture, this handy-sized guide covers a wide variety of topics, including beliefs and values, teens and *rumspringa,* clothing and transportation, children, the elderly, courtship and marriage, and shunning and discipline

◆ ◆ ◆ ◆ ◆

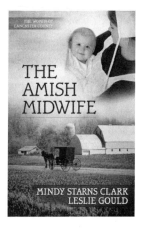

The Amish Midwife
Mindy Starns Clark and Leslie Gould

Winner of the 2012 Christy Award for Contemporary Series!

*A deathbed confession…a dusty carved box containing two locks of hair…a century-old letter about property in Switzerland…*Nurse-midwife Lexie Jaeger's encounter with all three rekindles a burning desire to meet her biological family. Propelled on a personal journey of discovery, Lexie's search for the truth takes her from Oregon to the heart of Pennsylvania's Amish country. There she finds Marta Bayer, a mysterious lay-midwife who may hold the key to Lexie's past. But Marta isn't talking, especially now that she has troubles of her own. As Lexie steps in to assume Marta's patient load and continues the search for her birth family, a handsome local doctor proves to be a welcome distraction. But will he also distract her from the man back home who awaits her return?

Will this woman who wants to control everything ever learn to "let be" and depend totally on God? Or will her stubborn determination to unearth the secrets of the past tear her newfound family apart?

◆ ◆ ◆ ◆ ◆

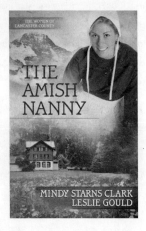

The Amish Nanny
Mindy Starns Clark and Leslie Gould

A cave behind a waterfall…a dying confession…a secret agreement hidden for a century… Amish-raised Ada Rupp knows nothing of these elements of her family's past. Instead, her eyes are fixed firmly on the future—for the first time in her life. With a serious medical issue behind her, Ada is eager to pursue her God-given gift of teaching at the local Amish school and her dream of marrying Will Gundy, a handsome widower she's loved since she was a child. But when both desires meet with unexpected obstacles, Ada's fragile heart grows heavy. Then she meets Daniel, an attractive Mennonite scholar with a surprising request. He needs her help—along with the help of Will's family—to save an important historic site.

Ada, a family friend, and a young child head to Switzerland to mend an old family rift and help preserve Ada's religious heritage. To save the site, Ada and Daniel must unlock secrets from the past. In doing so, will they discover they also have a future together…or will Ada's heart forever belong to Will?